iPhone 17 Pro

User Guide for Beginners and Seniors

Colaine Jobs

Published by
GRAPEVINE BOOKS

www.grapevinebooks.com
email: contact@grapevinebooks.com

Ordering Information:
Quantity sales: Special discounts are available on quantity purchases
by corporations, associations, and others.
For details, reach out to the publisher.

First published by Grapevine Books 2025

TABLE Of CONTENTS

How to Use This Guide

Welcome to your iPhone 17 Pro journey. Whether you're brand new to iPhones or upgrading from an older model, this guide is designed with you in mind. We'll walk you through each essential feature step by step, using simple language, clear visuals, and practical tips. No tech jargon. No rushing.

Each chapter focuses on something you'll actually use. Calling. Texting. Taking photos. Using maps. Setting up payments. Even troubleshooting issues that might pop up later. You don't have to read the book cover to cover. Jump to any chapter whenever you need help with a specific task. This guide is especially helpful for seniors and beginners who want confidence while learning. You'll find enlarged text, clean explanations, and reassuring encouragement along the way. There's also a glossary in the back for unfamiliar terms and quick reference charts for buttons, icons, and settings.

What You'll Need

- Your iPhone 17 Pro (charged and turned on)
- A comfortable place to sit and explore
- Wi-Fi connection (recommended but not required for all features)

Let's take it slow, one tap at a time. Your iPhone is powerful, but more importantly, it's yours. Let's make it work for you.

What's New in iPhone 17 Pro & iOS 26

The iPhone 17 Pro introduces powerful new features, many of which are designed to make everyday tasks faster, easier, and even more enjoyable. If you're upgrading from an older iPhone or switching from another smartphone, here are some exciting changes to look forward to:

1. The Action Button

On the side of your iPhone, just above the volume buttons, you'll find the new Action Button. Instead of only toggling silent mode, this button can now be customized to perform a variety of tasks. You can use it to open the camera, activate the flashlight, launch voice memos, or even run an accessibility shortcut. We'll show you how to set it up later in the book.

2. Dynamic Island

At the top of the screen, the Dynamic Island replaces the notch and gives you live information in a small, interactive space. You'll see real-time updates like timers, music playback, call duration, and directions without leaving your current app.

3. Apple Intelligence (AI)

With iOS 26, your iPhone can now summarize messages, suggest smart replies, help write or rewrite notes, and even use Genmoji, custom emojis created with your words. Apple Intelligence brings advanced AI to Siri, Messages, and more, making your phone more responsive and useful in real-world situations.

4. Smarter FaceTime Features

With the new 18MP Center Stage front camera, FaceTime video calls are now even better. The camera automatically adjusts to keep everyone centered in the shot during video calls, even if people move or join the conversation. You can also leave a FaceTime video message if someone misses your call. Plus, the AI-powered Live Translation feature can now automatically translate captions during calls, making it easier to communicate across languages.

5.Smarter Messaging Features

The Messages app has been upgraded with AI-powered writing tools that allow you to proofread your text, change the tone of your messages, or even summarize them. The app now supports Live Translation, so texts can be translated in real-time. You can also create custom emojis, called Genmoji, directly in the keyboard. Other helpful tools include the ability to create polls in group chats and use the new Check In feature to notify a friend or family member when you safely reach your destination.

6. Customization & Accessibility

With iOS 26, you can personalize your iPhone even more. The Lock Screen is fully customizable with widgets, new fonts, and even emoji wallpapers. Home Screen customization has also been improved, allowing for flexible app placement, custom widget stacks, and more. For accessibility, Live Speech lets you type messages that are read out loud during calls, and new Voice Control enhancements make it easier to navigate your phone hands-free. There are also improvements for people with visual or hearing impairments, such as Sound Recognition and Live Listen for better communication.

7. More Privacy, More Safety

Features like App Privacy Reports, Safety Check, and Lockdown Mode give you more control over your data. You can now review and change what apps know about you with a few quick taps. New microphone and camera indicators let you know when apps are using them, and you can easily manage permissions. Plus, End-to-End Encryption continues to protect iMessages and FaceTime calls, ensuring your conversations remain private.

Chapter 1: Getting Started

Unboxing Your iPhone 17 Pro

Your new iPhone 17 Pro arrives in a sleek, minimalist box. Inside, you'll find:

- The iPhone 17 Pro itself
- A USB-C to USB-C charging cable
- A small envelope containing a SIM tool (for physical SIM models), Apple logo sticker, and safety information

Note: Apple no longer includes a wall power adapter or headphones in the box. If you need those, you can use accessories from a previous iPhone or purchase compatible ones separately.

Before turning the phone on, take a moment to admire the design. The **iPhone 17 Pro** features a durable titanium frame, Ceramic Shield front, and a stunning edge-to-edge display. With its sleek, modern design and advanced materials, the iPhone 17 Pro is as beautiful as it is powerful.

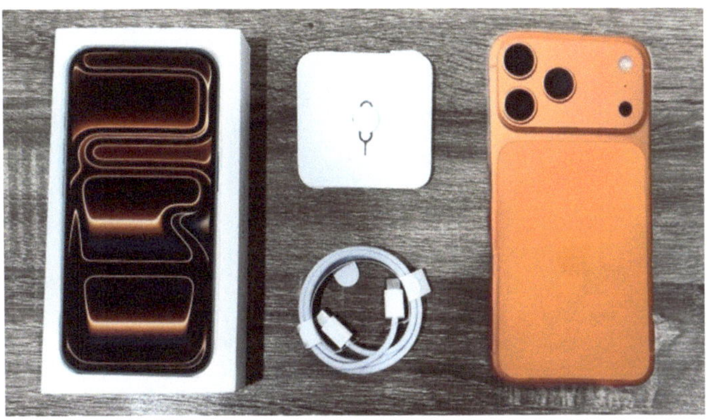

Exploring the Buttons and Ports

Let's get familiar with the outside of your phone:

Power Button (Right Side): Press and hold to turn your iPhone on or off. Also used for Apple Pay and Siri.

Volume Buttons (Left Side): Increase or decrease sound. Can also be used to take photos when the Camera is open.

Action Button (Above Volume Buttons): A customizable button that replaces the old silent/ring switch.

USB-C Port (Bottom Center): Used for charging and connecting to accessories.

Speaker and Microphone (Bottom): For phone calls, music, and Siri.

Face ID Camera (Top Front): Works with the TrueDepth system to recognize your face and unlock your phone.

Rear Cameras (Back): Includes ultra-wide, wide, and telephoto lenses.

Now that you've unboxed and identified all the main parts, it's time to turn it on and begin setup.

First-Time Setup Made Simple

Press and hold the **Power Button** on the right side of your iPhone until the Apple logo appears. After a few seconds, you'll see the "Hello" screen. Here's what to do next:

Swipe Up to Begin

Follow the on-screen prompts to choose your language and country or region.

Connect to Wi-Fi

Choose your home Wi-Fi network and enter the password. A connection is needed to activate your phone and set up certain features.

Set Up Face ID

Hold your phone about 12 inches from your face. Move your head slowly in a circle so the camera can capture your face from all angles. You can skip this step and set it up later if you prefer.

Create a Passcode

Choose a six-digit passcode to protect your phone. You'll use it as a backup if Face ID doesn't work or if your phone restarts.

Sign In with Your Apple ID

If you already have one, enter your Apple ID and password. If not, tap "Forgot password or don't have an Apple ID?" and follow the steps to create one. This account lets you use iCloud, the App Store, FaceTime, iMessage, and more.

Restore or Transfer Data

If you're upgrading from another iPhone or Android, choose one of the data transfer options. You can also start fresh with no previous content.

Customize Settings

You'll be guided through privacy settings, Siri activation, app permissions, and screen time preferences. Most settings can be changed later if needed.

Welcome to iPhone

Once setup is complete, your iPhone will show the Home Screen. You're ready to explore.

Setting Up Face ID & Apple ID

Both Face ID and Apple ID are key to making your iPhone experience smooth and secure. Let's walk through how they work and why they matter.

Face ID:
Your Face Is Your Password.

What it does: Face ID unlocks your iPhone, authorizes App Store purchases, logs into apps, and confirms payments just by recognizing your face.

How to set it up or redo it:

1. Open **Settings**
2. Tap **Face ID** & **Passcode**
3. Enter your passcode
4. Tap **Set Up Face ID**
5. Position your face inside the circle and slowly move your head in a circle to complete the scan
6. Repeat once more for a second scan
7. Done!

Face ID works best when your face is fully visible. It also adapts to gradual changes like glasses or facial hair over time. If you're wearing a mask or want another trusted person to access the phone, you can set up an alternate appearance.

Apple ID: The Key to Everything Apple

Your Apple ID is your digital passport for everything on your iPhone. It lets you use iCloud, download apps, sync messages, store photos, and more.

If you skipped Apple ID setup earlier, here's how to do it:

1. Go to **Settings**
2. Tap **Sign in to your iPhone** at the top
3. Enter your Apple ID and password or create a new one
4. Follow the prompts to verify your email and accept terms

Be sure to use a strong password and set up two-factor authentication for extra protection.

Tip: Your Apple ID also helps you locate a lost iPhone, back up your data, and protect your purchases.

Charging Your iPhone & Battery Basics

The iPhone 16 Pro uses a USB-C port for charging and data transfer, replacing the old Lightning connector. Charging your phone is easy, but there are a few helpful things to know for keeping your battery healthy.

How to Charge Your iPhone

1. Plug the included **USB-C to USB-C cable** into your iPhone.
2. Connect the other end to a USB-C power adapter (20W or higher is recommended).
3. Plug the adapter into a wall outlet.
4. A lightning bolt icon will appear on the battery symbol in the top corner, confirming that it's charging.

If you want to charge wirelessly, place your iPhone face up on any **MagSafe or Qi-compatible** charging pad. It will automatically align and begin charging.

Battery Health Tips

- **Keep it between 20% and 80%:** Charging to 100% or letting it drain to 0% every time wears the battery faster over time.

- **Use Optimized Battery Charging:** This feature learns your charging habits and slows charging past 80% until you need it. It's on by default.
- **Avoid extreme heat or cold:** Charging in hot environments can damage your battery long-term.
- **Check battery health anytime:** Go to Settings > Battery > Battery Health & Charging. Look for Maximum Capacity and Peak Performance Capability

If your battery is draining quickly, don't worry. We'll cover power-saving settings and performance tips later in the book.

Chapter 2: Mastering the Basics

Using Touch Gestures with Confidence

The iPhone 17 Pro does not have a physical home button. Instead, it relies entirely on touch gestures that are easy to learn. Once you get used to them, they'll feel second nature.

Here are the most important gestures:

- **Swipe Up from the Bottom:** Go to the Home Screen from any app. Think of this as your new Home button.
- **Swipe Up and Hold:** View all open apps. This is called the App Switcher. Swipe side to side to see your running apps, and swipe up on any one to close it.
- **Swipe Down from the Top Right:** Open the Control Center, where you'll find quick tools like Wi-Fi, flashlight, screen brightness, and volume.
- **Swipe Down from the Center or Top Left:** Access Notifications such as missed calls, messages, and reminders.
- **Tap and Hold:** Press firmly and hold an icon to open extra options. This works on apps, links, and photos. On the Home Screen, this gesture also lets you move or delete apps.
- **Pinch to Zoom :** Place two fingers on the screen and move them apart to zoom in. Move them together to zoom out. Great for viewing photos, web pages, and maps.

These gestures may feel unfamiliar at first, but don't worry. Try practicing a few times. There's no rush, and you can't break anything by exploring.

Making and Receiving Calls

Your iPhone 17 Pro makes calling easy, whether you're dialing a number by hand, selecting a contact, or answering a call that comes in.

To Make a Call

- Open the **Phone** app (green icon with a white phone).

- Tap the **Keypad** tab to dial a number manually.
- Tap the **Contacts** tab to find someone saved in your phonebook.
- Tap the **Favorites** tab to access people you call often.
- After entering or selecting a number, tap the **green call button**.

Tip: You can also tap and hold the Action Button (if customized) or ask Siri to call someone by name. Example: "Call Sarah."

To Answer a Call

- If the screen is **on**: Tap **Accept** or **Decline**.
- If the screen is **locked**: Swipe the **green phone icon** to the right to answer. To decline a call from the lock screen, press the **Side button** twice.
- Tap **Remind Me** or **Message** if you can't talk right now.

To Reject a Call with a Text Message

If you can't talk, select the Message icon, then select a preset message. You can also tap Custom... to create and send a custom message.

Ask Reason for Calling

You can screen unknown callers by enabling the Ask Reason for Calling feature. When an unknown number calls, your iPhone answers automatically, and Siri asks the caller for the reason. The caller's response is transcribed to text and displayed on your screen, allowing you to decide whether to answer, decline, or send a reply. To enable this feature, go to **Settings** > **Phone** > **Screen Unknown Callers** and select **Ask Reason for Calling**.

Alternative Options for Screening Unknown Callers

If you prefer not to use Ask Reason for Calling, you have two other options:

- **Silence**: Automatically sends calls from unrecognized numbers to voicemail.
- **Never**: Allows calls from unknown numbers to ring normally, just like calls from saved contacts.

To switch between these options, go to **Settings** > **Phone** > **Screen Unknown Callers** and select your preferred choice.

During a Call

Once the call is active, you'll see options like:

- **Mute:** Silences your microphone
- **Keypad:** Dial numbers during the call
- **Speaker:** Switches to speakerphone
- **Add Call:** Starts a conference call
- **FaceTime:** Switches to video call if available

You can also adjust the volume using the side buttons during a call.

Sending Text Messages & Emojis

Texting with your iPhone 17 Pro is easy and fun. You can send plain messages, photos, voice recordings, emojis, and more using the built-in **Messages** app.

To Send a Text Message

1. Open the **Messages** app (green icon with a white speech bubble).
2. Tap the **Compose** button in the top right corner (a square with a pencil).
3. In the **To**: field, type the name or number of the person you want to message.
4. Tap the **text field** at the bottom and begin typing.
5. Tap the **Send** button (blue or green arrow) to deliver your message.

Blue vs. Green Bubbles

- **Blue bubble:** Sent via iMessage (Apple's system, internet-based).
- **Green bubble:** Sent as a regular SMS text (carrier-based).

You can send iMessages only to other Apple users. Messages between Apple **and non-Apple devices will appear in green.**

Adding Emojis

1. Tap the **smiley face** icon on the keyboard to open the emoji panel.
2. Browse categories or use the **search bar**.
3. Tap any emoji to insert it into your message.
4. Tap the **ABC key** to return to the regular keyboard.

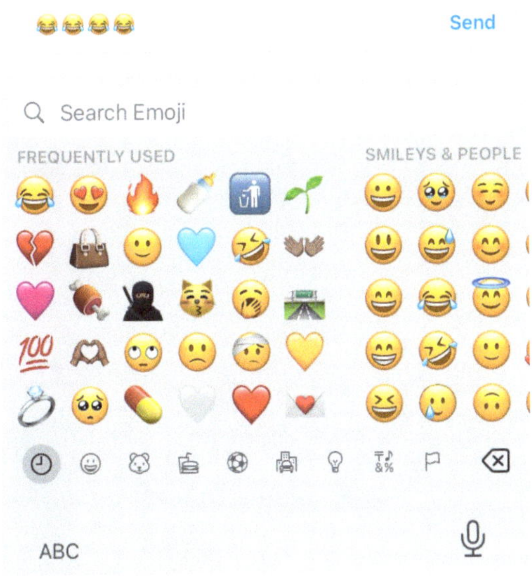

Genmoji: Use Apple Intelligence to create custom emojis directly in your messages. Simply type a description, and Genmoji will generate an emoji that matches it.

Using Genmoji

1. Go to a text field (like in **Messages** or any app where you can type).
2. Tap the emoji key on the keyboard.
3. Tap the **Genmoji icon** (a pink and blue smiley with a plus sign) in the top right corner of the keyboard.
4. You can either:

- **Type a prompt** to describe the emoji you want to create (e.g., “happy cat” or “sunset”)
- Tap **"Choose Person"** to create a Genmoji of yourself or someone from your photo library.

5. Swipe through the generated options and select the one you like.
6. Tap "**Add**" to insert it into your message or tap the **send button** to send it.

Sending a Photo or Video

1. Tap the **camera** icon next to the message field.
2. Choose **Take Photo** or **Choose** from Library.
3. Tap **Send** once you've selected your photo or video.

Sending Voice Messages

1. Tap and hold the **audio wave icon** on the right side of the text field.
2. Speak clearly into the microphone.
3. Release to stop recording.
4. Tap **Send** or **Cancel**.

This feature is especially helpful for quick replies or if typing is uncomfortable.

Using Voice Dictation & the Keyboard

Typing on the iPhone keyboard is easy, but sometimes you may prefer to speak instead. Your iPhone 17 Pro gives you the choice to either type with your fingers or speak using voice dictation, now enhanced by Apple Intelligence for better accuracy and recognition.

Typing with the On-Screen Keyboard

Whenever you tap a text box (like in **Messages**, **Notes**, or **Safari**), the keyboard appears automatically. Here's what you'll see:

- **Letters and Numbers:** Standard QWERTY layout
- **Emoji Key:** Smiley face icon for emojis
- **Microphone Key:** Used to activate voice dictation
- **123 Key:** Switches to numbers and symbols
- **Globe Key:** Changes keyboard language if you've added others
- **Space Bar and Return Key:** For normal typing and starting new lines

You can tap and hold certain keys (like letters or punctuation) to see more options, such as accented characters or alternate symbols.

Using Voice Dictation

Voice dictation lets you speak instead of type, and your iPhone will convert your words into text.

To use dictation:

- Tap any text box to bring up the keyboard.
- Tap the **microphone icon** on the bottom right of the keyboard.
- Speak clearly and naturally. You can say punctuation, such as "comma" or "period," as you talk.
- Tap the **keyboard icon** again when you're done speaking.

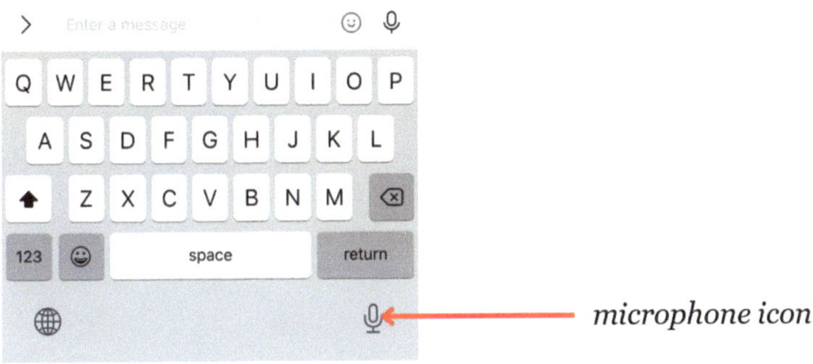

Example:
Say "Hello comma how are you question mark"
Your phone will type:
Hello, how are you?

Tips for Better Dictation

- Speak clearly, but naturally; no need to talk like a robot.
- Pause briefly between sentences.
- Review the text afterward in case you want to edit anything manually.
- Use dictation in any app where the keyboard appears, including Messages, Notes, Email, and Safari.

Voice dictation is especially helpful if typing feels difficult or slow. With just your voice, you can send full messages, take notes, or write emails with ease.

Adding Contacts Easily

Saving people's phone numbers in your Contacts app helps you call, message, and identify callers quickly. Once a number is saved, you don't have to remember it. Just tap the person's name.

To Add a New Contact

1. Open the **Phone** app.
2. Tap the **Contacts** tab at the bottom.
3. Tap the **plus sign** (+) in the top right corner.
4. Enter the person's details:

- **First and Last Name**
- **Phone Number**
- **Email Address** (optional)
- **Company Name** (optional)
- **Birthday or Notes** (optional)

5. Tap **Done** in the top right when finished.

You can also add a photo for each contact. Just tap **Add Photo** to use your camera or choose one from your library.

To Edit or Delete a Contact

1. Go to **Contacts** and tap the person's name.
2. Tap **Edit** in the top right corner.
3. Make changes, then tap **Done**.
4. To delete, scroll to the bottom and tap **Delete Contact**.

Other Ways to Add Contacts

- **From a Call:** After a call with a new number, go to the Recents tab, tap the "**i**" **icon**, and choose **Create New Contact** or **Add to Existing**.
- **From a Message:** Tap the number at the top of a conversation and select **Add Contact**.

Contact Posters

In addition to saving basic contact information, you can create a personalized Contact Poster that will be displayed when others receive your calls.

To Create or Edit a Contact Poster

1. Open the **Phone** app.
2. Tap the **Contacts** tab at the bottom.
3. Select **My Card** at the top of the screen.

4. Tap **Edit** in the top right corner.
5. Add a photo, customize fonts, and choose how you appear to others.
6. Tap **Done** when finished.

Saving contacts keeps your phone organized and lets you use features like **Favorites**, **Do Not Disturb exceptions**, and **Emergency Bypass**.

Chapter 3: Personalizing Your iPhone

Changing Wallpaper & Display Zoom

Your iPhone should feel like yours, from the moment you wake the screen. Customizing your wallpaper and adjusting how large everything appears can make your phone easier to use and more enjoyable.

How to Change Your Wallpaper

1. Open the **Settings** app.
2. Tap **Wallpaper**.
3. Tap **Add New Wallpaper**.
4. Choose from options like:

- Apple's built-in wallpapers (dynamic, astronomy, emoji)
- A photo from your gallery
- A gradient or color background

5. Tap **Set as Wallpaper Pair** to use the same image for your Lock Screen and Home Screen, or choose each separately.

You can preview how it looks before finalizing. Live wallpapers (like the weather or your current location) will animate when you wake your phone.

Adjusting Display Zoom and Text Size

If things look too small or hard to tap, try these settings:

To make app icons and text larger:

1. Go to **Settings** > **Display & Brightness**
2. Tap **Display Zoom**
3. Choose **Standard** or **Larger Text**
4. Tap **Done**, then your phone will restart with the new layout

To adjust text size only:

1. Go to **Settings** > **Accessibility** > **Display & Text Size**
2. Tap **Larger Text**
3. Drag the slider to increase font size

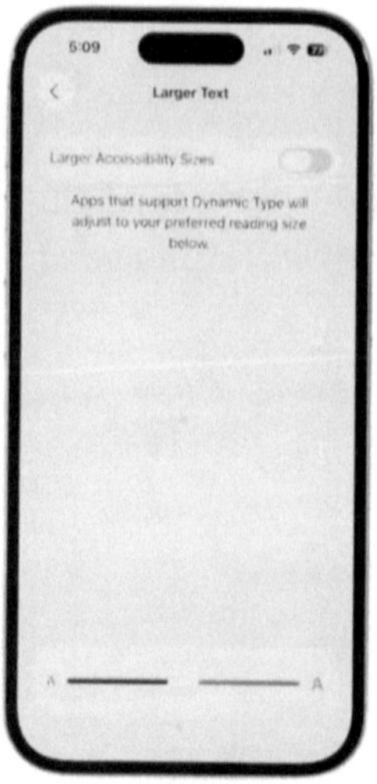

For even larger sizes, go to:
Settings > **Accessibility** > **Display & Text Size** > **Larger Text**
Turn on **Larger Accessibility Sizes** and move the slider to your comfort level.

This change applies to system menus, messages, and apps that support dynamic text.

Making Icons Bigger and More Spaced Out

Want a cleaner Home Screen with fewer apps and bigger icons?

1. Go to **Settings** > **Display & Brightness**
2. Scroll down and tap **Display Zoom**
3. Select **Larger Text** (this also increases icon size and spacing)
4. Tap **Done** and allow the phone to restart

The layout will now appear more spacious and easier to see.

Removing Clutter from the Home Screen

You don't need to keep every app on your main screens. To simplify your layout:

- **Tap and hold** on any app until the icons jiggle
- Tap the **minus sign** to remove it from the Home Screen (this won't delete the app; it stays in the App Library)
- Drag apps to group them into folders if you want better organization

You're in control of how your phone looks and feels. The goal is comfort and clarity, not perfection.

Organizing Apps with Folders & Widgets

As you download more apps, your Home Screen can quickly become cluttered. Thankfully, your iPhone 17 Pro makes it easy to group apps into folders and add helpful widgets to stay organized.

Creating App Folders

1. Tap and hold any app icon until it starts to jiggle.
2. Drag the app on top of another app you want in the same folder.
3. A folder will automatically be created with both apps inside.
4. Tap the **folder name** to rename it (e.g., "Games," "Health," "Social").
5. Drag in more apps if you'd like.
6. Tap **Done** in the top right when finished.

Folders help keep your Home Screen neat and make it easier to find what you need.

Adding and Using Widgets

Widgets show live information, like weather, calendar events, battery life, or news, right on your Home Screen.

To add a widget:

1. Tap and hold on any empty space on the Home Screen until the icons jiggle.
2. Tap the **plus sign** (+) in the top left corner.
3. Scroll through the list of available widgets.
4. Tap a widget to preview sizes (small, medium, large).
5. Tap Add **Widget** to place it on your screen.
6. Move it where you want, then tap Done.

Widgets can go between apps, above them, or take up an entire row. You can even **stack multiple widgets** together to swipe through them (called a Smart Stack).

Widgets on your **iPhone 17 Pro** allow even more customization. You can change the widget's style, choosing from light, dark, clear, or tinted options, and adjust the size to fit your layout. Additionally, you can add widgets to your Lock Screen, displaying quick info like weather or activity, directly below the time for easy access.

Interactive widgets let you take action directly from the Home or Lock Screen. For example, you can play podcasts, control smart home devices, or check your calendar without even opening the app. Widgets can also change based on your **Focus mode**, showing personalized views depending on your activity or location.

Notes widget

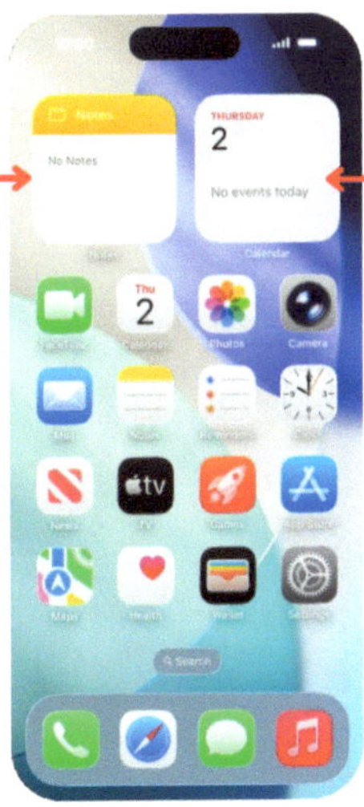

Calendar widget

Well-organized screens save time and reduce stress. The more your layout works for you, the more confident you'll feel using your phone every day.

Focus Modes & Notification Control

Focus Modes help you stay in control of your time by filtering which notifications and apps can reach you during specific moments, like sleeping, working, relaxing, or driving. With the **iPhone 17 Pro** running **iOS 26**, Focus modes are more powerful and customizable, thanks to the integration of **Apple Intelligence**.

Setting Up a Focus Mode

1. Open **Settings**
2. Tap **Focus**
3. Choose a preset (Sleep, Work, Personal, etc.) or tap **Add Focus** to create a custom one
4. Select:

- **Allowed People:** Choose who can call or message you during this Focus
- **Allowed Apps:** Pick apps that can send notifications
- **Home Screen & Lock Screen Options:** Customize how your screen looks when the Focus is on
- **Schedule or Automation:** Set times, locations, or app triggers to turn it on automatically

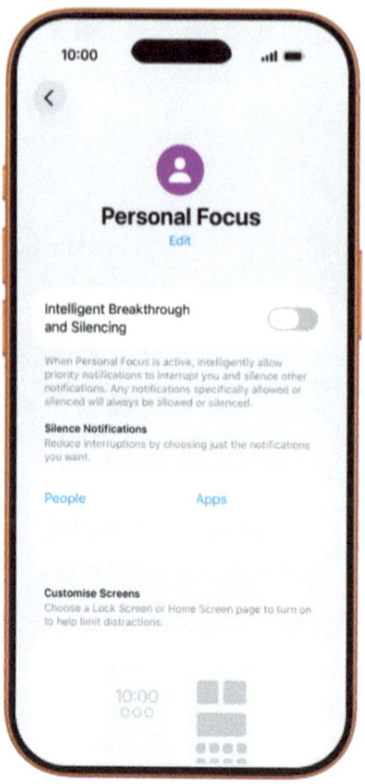

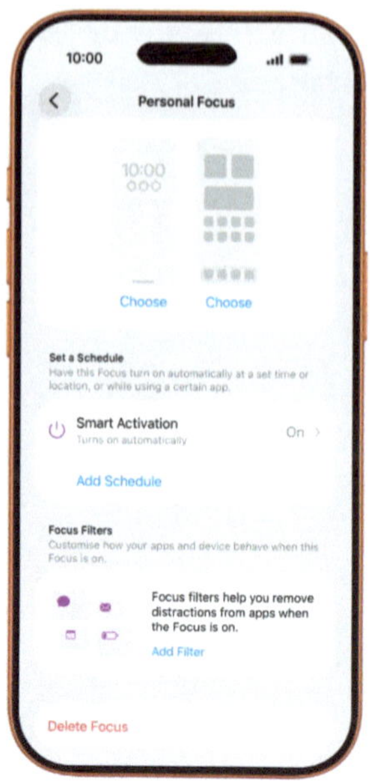

You'll see a moon, work briefcase, or other icon in the status bar when a Focus is active.

Focus Mode Enhancements

- **Reduce Interruptions**: AI filters notifications, ensuring only urgent alerts come through during Focus mode.
- **Focus Filters**: Customize app content (e.g., **Calendar**, **Safari** tab groups) and system settings (e.g., **Dark Mode**, **Always-On Display**) for a personalized experience.

Switching Focus Modes Quickly

- Swipe down from the **top right corner** to open **Control Center**.
- Tap the **Focus button** (moon icon or other symbol), then choose which Focus to turn on or off.

You can also long-press it for more options, like turning on until you leave a location or for just one hour.

Managing Notifications in General

To control how and when apps alert you:

1. Go to **Settings** > **Notifications**
2. Tap any app to:

- Allow or block notifications
- Choose banner style (temporary or persistent)
- Set sound or vibration preferences
- Show previews or hide them when locked

You can also enable **Scheduled Summary** to group less urgent notifications into a daily bundle; it is especially helpful for reducing distractions.

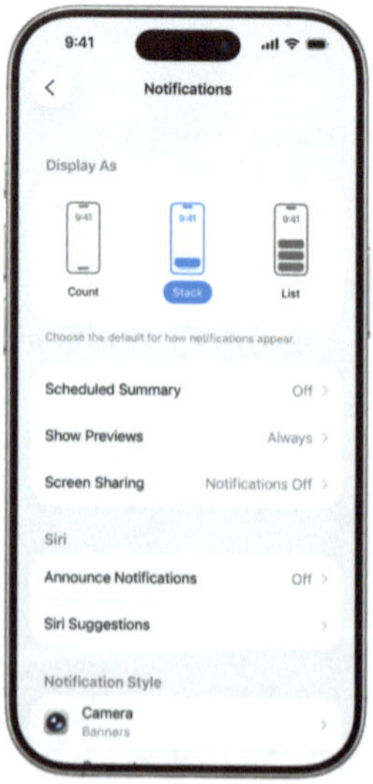

Customizing the Action Button

The iPhone 17 Pro introduces a brand-new **Action Button;** a physical button on the side of your phone that replaces the old ring/silent switch. By default, it toggles between silent and ring mode, but with a few taps in Settings, you can customize it to perform various tasks.

Where to Find It

Look at the **left side** of your iPhone, just above the volume buttons. That small button is the Action Button.

By default, it switches between silent and ring mode, but with a few taps in Settings, you can assign it a different task.

How to Customize the Action Button

1. Open **Settings**
2. Tap **Action Button**
3. Swipe left or right through the available actions
4. Choose what you want the button to do

Options include:

- **Silent Mode** (default)
- **Focus Mode**
- **Camera**
- **Flashlight**
- **Voice Memo**
- **Magnifier**
- **Translate**
- **Shortcut** (lets you run any Shortcuts you've created)
- **Accessibility Features** like VoiceOver or AssistiveTouch

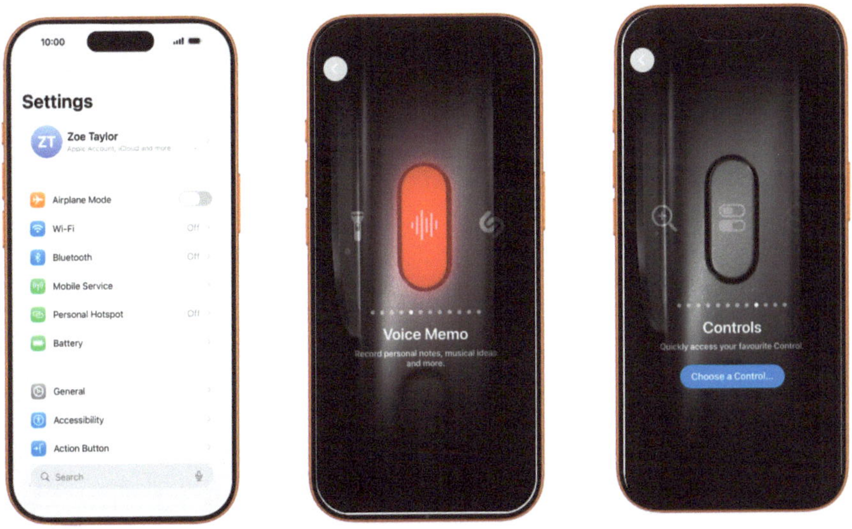

The **Action Button** can now trigger more advanced **Apple Intelligence** features like **Live Translation**, making it even more versatile in real-world situations.

How to Use It

Press and hold the Action Button to trigger its assigned action. For example, if you set it to **Camera**, holding the button will instantly open the camera, even if your iPhone is locked.

This button is especially helpful for quick access to tools you use often. You can change its function anytime based on your needs.

Chapter 4: Photos, Camera & FaceTime

Taking Great Photos & Portraits

Your iPhone 17 Pro has one of the most advanced cameras ever put into a phone. Whether you're snapping casual moments or capturing special events, the Camera app helps you take clear, vibrant photos with just a tap.

Opening the Camera

- **From the Lock Screen:** Swipe left
- **From the Home Screen:** Tap the Camera app
- **Using the Action Button:** If set to Camera, press and hold
- **Ask Siri:** Say "Open Camera"

Using the Basic Camera Modes

At the bottom of the screen (or side, if you're holding it horizontally), you'll see different shooting modes:

- **Photo** (default): For regular pictures
- **Portrait**: Adds a soft, blurred background for more professional-looking shots. Perfect for people, pets, or any subject where you want a sharp focus and a soft background. After taking a portrait, you can even adjust the blur level and lighting effects to make it just right.
- **Video**: For filming
- **Cinematic**: Creates a movie-style focus effect while recording
- **Pano**: For wide panoramic shots
- **Slo-Mo and Time-Lapse**: For creative video effects

Swipe left or right to switch between modes.

Panoramic (pano) shot

Taking a Photo with Dual Capture

The iPhone 17 Pro lets you use Dual Capture to record with both the front and rear cameras simultaneously. This is perfect for capturing both yourself and your surroundings in the same shot, making it ideal for video messages, group shots, or creative selfies.

Better Photos

- **Center Stage for Selfies**: The **front** camera automatically adjusts to keep everyone in the shot, even if you move. This makes group selfies much easier to take without stretching your arm.

- **Zooming in on Details**: The iPhone 17 Pro offers **4x** zoom for closer shots without losing quality. You can also use digital zoom for even closer views, up to **8x**.
- **Better Photos in Low Light**: The camera's new telephoto sensor helps take clearer, brighter pictures in low light, so you get great photos even when it's dark.
- **Macro Mode for Close-Up Shots**: When you take close-up photos, the camera automatically switches to **macro mode** to capture tiny details with sharp focus.
- **Get Creative with AI**: The camera's AI tools let you play with your photos, like animating them or creating new images based on prompts, for fun and creative results.

Taking a Photo

1. Frame your subject using the screen as a viewfinder
2. Tap the **shutter button** (big white circle)
3. Your photo is automatically saved to the **Photos** app

You can also:

- **Tap the screen** to adjust focus
- **Pinch to zoom** in or out
- **Tap and hold** the shutter for burst photos
- Use the **Volume Up** button to take a picture like a physical camera

Portrait Mode is perfect for people, pets, or any subject where you want a sharp focus and a soft background. After taking a portrait, you can even adjust the blur level and lighting effects.

Smart HDR, Night Mode & Depth Control

Your iPhone 17 Pro doesn't just take photos; it thinks about lighting, detail, and balance to give you the best shot every time. Here's how three key features work behind the scenes, and how you can use them to your advantage.

Smart HDR (High Dynamic Range)

Smart HDR automatically balances the bright and dark parts of a photo so everything looks natural and clear.

When it helps:

- Taking photos in sunlight or shadows
- Capturing sky details while keeping people visible
- Photographing high-contrast scenes

You don't need to turn it on; it's always working. But if you want to toggle it manually:

1. Go to **Settings** > **Camera**
2. Tap **Smart HDR** to turn it on or off

Night Mode

Night Mode helps you take clear, bright photos in low light without using a flash. It activates automatically when your iPhone senses dark conditions.

When Night Mode is on, a small yellow moon icon appears at the top of the screen.

To use it:

1. Hold your phone steady
2. Tap the shutter button
3. A timer will count down automatically (1 to 3 seconds, or longer for very dark scenes)
4. The camera will capture more light for a brighter photo

You can adjust the exposure time by tapping the moon icon and dragging the slider.

Tip: For best results, prop your phone on a table or use both hands to avoid blur.

Depth Control in Portrait Mode

After taking a portrait photo, you can control how blurry the background is, just like with a professional camera.

To adjust depth:

1. Open the **Photos** app
2. Tap on your portrait photo
3. Tap **Edit**
4. Use the **Depth slider** to increase or reduce the background blur
5. Tap **Done** to save changes

This is great for making your subject stand out or creating a more subtle effect depending on the setting.

Portrait Features:

- **Post-Capture Depth Adjustment**: Adjust the background blur (bokeh) after taking the photo, even in standard photo mode, thanks to **built-in depth mapping**.
- **Camera Control Slider**: In the **Camera app**, adjust **Exposure**, **Depth**, **Zoom**, **Styles**, and **Tone** for professional-level control.
- **Next-Gen Portraits**: Enhanced processing for more natural and detailed depth effects.

Viewing, Editing & Sharing Photos

Once you've captured your moments, the Photos app helps you find them, clean them up, and share them with ease. It organizes all your pictures and videos automatically, making it easy to enjoy and manage your memories.

Viewing Your Photos

1. Open the **Photos** app

2. Tap **Library** at the bottom
3. Choose **Years**, **Months**, **Days**, or **All Photos** to browse

Tap any image to view it full screen. Swipe left or right to go through your photo stream.

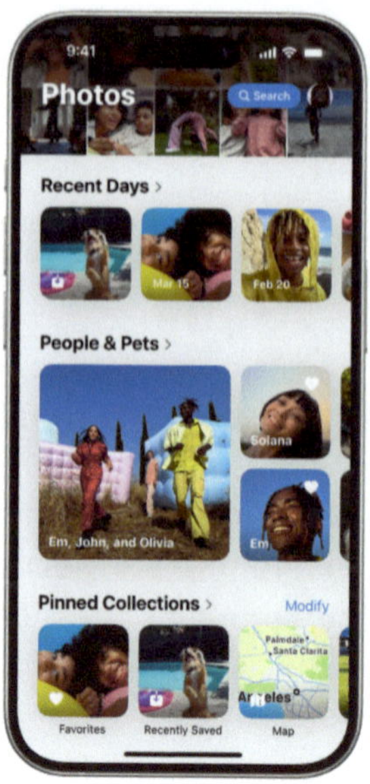

Editing a Photo

You can brighten a dark photo, crop it, or add filters with just a few taps:

1. Open the Photos app and tap a photo
2. Tap Edit in the top right corner
3. Use the adjustment icons at the bottom:

- **Auto-Enhance (magic wand icon):** Improves lighting and color
- **Exposure, Contrast, Brightness, etc.:** Fine-tune your image
- **Filters:** Add artistic color effects
- **Crop and Rotate:** Straighten or resize the photo

4. Tap **Done** to save your edits

Enhance Your Editing

- **Post-Capture Depth & Focus**: Adjust background blur and focus on any portrait photo after taking it.
- **Real-Time Depth Control**: Use the **Camera Control slider** to adjust blur in real-time for perfect focus.
- **Photographic Styles:** Apply built-in styles like **Rich Contrast** or **Vibrant** before shooting, saving you time on edits later.

Don't worry, you can always revert to the original image by opening the photo, tapping Edit, then tapping Revert.

Sharing a Photo

1. Tap any photo
2. Tap the Share icon (a box with an arrow pointing up)
3. Choose how to send it:

- **Messages**
- **Mail**
- **AirDrop**
- **Social media apps**

4. You can also print or save it to Files from this menu

You can share multiple photos by tapping Select, choosing several, then tapping Share.

Enhance Your Sharing

- **Shared Library**: Add photos automatically to a shared album with iCloud.
- **Share Automatically**: Set up your phone to add photos to shared albums as you take them.
- **Shared Albums**: Create albums for family and friends to view, like, and add their photos.
- **High-Res Photos**: The iPhone 17 Pro captures sharp 24MP photos, ensuring your images look great when shared.

Photos are more than images; they're memories. With just a little practice, you'll be able to enhance, enjoy, and share them like a pro.

Using FaceTime for Video Calls

FaceTime lets you have live, face-to-face video conversations with friends and family, wherever they are. All you need is a Wi-Fi or cellular connection and an Apple device on both ends.

Starting a FaceTime Call

1. Open the **FaceTime app** (green icon with a white video camera)
2. Tap **New FaceTime**
3. Type the name, phone number, or email of the person you want to call
4. Tap the **FaceTime button** (video icon) to start the call

If the person has an iPhone, iPad, or Mac, they'll receive the call. If not, you'll be notified that FaceTime isn't available.

During the Call

Once the call connects, you'll see the other person on screen and yourself in a small window. While on the call, you can:

- Tap the screen to show call options
- Mute your microphone
- Flip the camera to show the other side
- Add **effects** like **stickers**, **reactions**, or **Memoji**
- Tap anywhere to bring the controls back if they disappear

Leaving a FaceTime Video Message

If the person doesn't answer, you can now leave a short video message.

1. After the missed call screen appears, tap **Record Video**
2. Say your message
3. Tap **Send** or **Cancel**

This works just like leaving a voicemail, but with video.

Making Group FaceTime Calls

You can also FaceTime with more than one person at once.

1. Open FaceTime
2. Tap **New FaceTime**
3. Add multiple contacts
4. Tap the **video icon** to begin the group call

Everyone can join and leave freely, and their video tiles resize automatically as they speak.

FaceTime Messages & Reactions

FaceTime in iOS 26 isn't just about seeing someone's face. It now includes fun ways to express yourself, whether the person answers or not.

Leave a FaceTime Message

If your call isn't answered, you can now leave a short video or audio message, just like leaving a voicemail.

To leave a message:

1. Wait for the call to ring and go unanswered
2. On the screen that appears, tap **Record Video**
3. Say your message, then tap **Send**

The recipient will get it in their **FaceTime app** and can watch it anytime. This is especially helpful for quick check-ins or sending a smile when you can't connect live.

Using Reactions in Live FaceTime Calls

Apple has added animated reactions that appear on screen during video calls, adding more emotion and fun to your chats.

To trigger a reaction:

Use simple hand gestures during a FaceTime call:

- **Thumbs-up:** Triggers floating thumbs
- **Two thumbs-up:** Fireworks
- **Peace sign (two fingers):** Balloons
- **Heart gesture:** Red hearts
- **Thumbs-down:** Shows thumbs-down icons

Reactions work automatically as long as Video Effects are turned on in Control Center.

How to Turn Video Effects On or Off

1. Open **Control Center** while on a FaceTime call (swipe down from top right)
2. Tap **Video Effects**
3. Toggle on or off as needed

These reactions make conversations more expressive, especially for birthdays, good news, or silly moments.

Chapter 5: Staying Connected

Setting Up Email Step-by-Step

Your iPhone 17 Pro lets you manage email easily using the built-in Mail app. Whether you use Gmail, iCloud, Yahoo, Outlook, or another service, setting it up takes just a few steps.

Add an Email Account

1. Open the **Settings** app
2. Scroll down and tap **Mail**
3. Tap **Accounts**
4. Tap **Add Account**
5. Choose your email provider (Gmail, Outlook, Yahoo, etc.)
6. Enter your email address and password
7. Follow the on-screen prompts to finish setup

If your provider isn't listed, choose Other and enter your details manually.

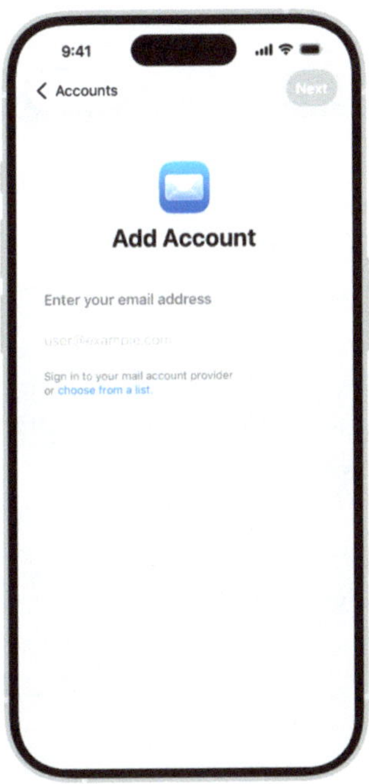

Using the Mail App

Once your account is added:

1. Open the **Mail** app (white envelope on blue background)
2. Tap **Inbox** to see new messages
3. Tap an email to open and read
4. Use the icons at the bottom to:

- **Reply** or **forward**
- **Move to trash**
- **Flag** for follow-up
- **Archive or move** to a folder

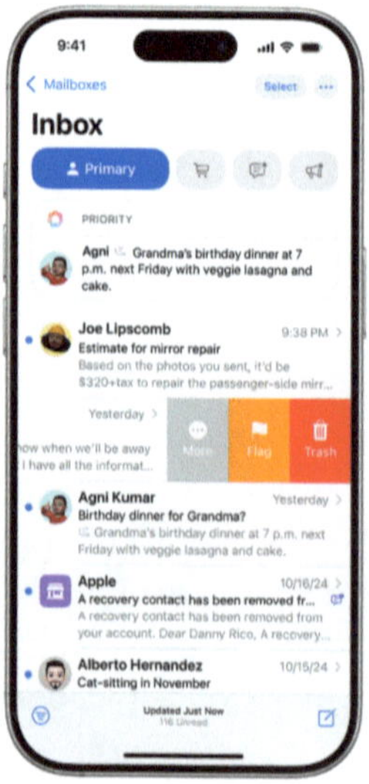

Pull down on the inbox to refresh your email.

Composing a New Email

1. Tap the **Compose** button (square with pencil) in the bottom right
2. Enter the recipient's email address
3. Type a subject and your message
4. Tap **Send** (upward arrow)

You can also attach photos or documents by tapping inside the message and selecting **Insert Photo or Attachment.**

Tip: If you use multiple email accounts, you can switch between them inside the Mail app by tapping Mailboxes and selecting the one you want. If you want to avoid interruptions during certain times, Focus modes can help manage notifications so you only get the most important emails.

Social Media Basics: Facebook, WhatsApp, etc.

Social media apps help you stay connected with friends, family, and communities all over the world. Your iPhone 17 Pro makes it easy to download, set up, and use the most popular ones, whether you're posting photos, joining group chats, or just browsing updates.

Downloading Social Media Apps

1. Open the **App Store** (blue icon with a white "A")
2. Tap **Search** at the bottom
3. Type the name of the app (e.g., Facebook, WhatsApp, Instagram)
4. Tap **Get** next to the correct result
5. Use **Face ID** or your **Apple ID password** to download

The app will appear on your Home Screen once installed.

Setting Up Facebook

1. Open the **Facebook app**
2. Tap **Log In** or **Create New Account**
3. Follow the instructions to add your name, email or phone, and password
4. Add a profile photo and a few details if you like
5. Start browsing posts, adding friends, and commenting

You'll see a **News Feed**, **Notifications**, and a **Menu** where you can adjust settings and privacy.

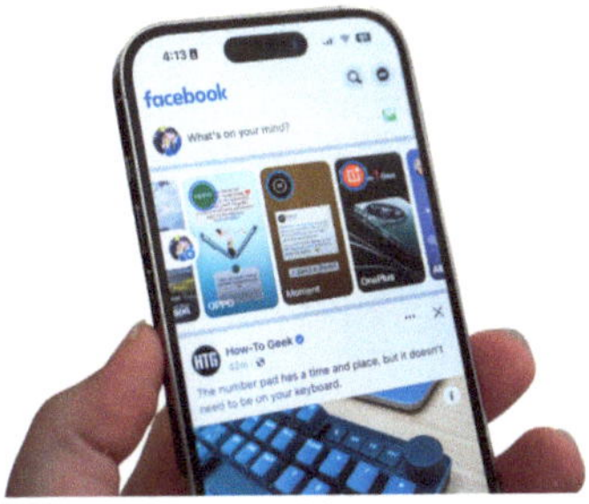

Using WhatsApp

WhatsApp is a free, secure messaging app used around the world.

1. Open the **WhatsApp app**
2. Enter your phone number
3. Verify using a code sent by text
4. Add your name and a profile picture
5. Tap the **Chat tab** to message contacts who also use WhatsApp

You can send text messages, voice recordings, pictures, videos, and even make video or voice calls.

Other Popular Apps

- **Instagram:** Share photos and videos, follow friends, and explore interests
- **Messenger:** Facebook's chat app for direct messages
- **YouTube:** Watch and share videos, subscribe to channels
- **Nextdoor:** Connect with neighbors and local services
- **X (formerly Twitter):** Read and share short messages and news updates

Each app has its own look, but they all include simple buttons for posting, reacting, and messaging. You can always adjust **notification settings** to reduce distractions.

The larger battery allows you to stay connected, create, and share content all day without needing to charge constantly.

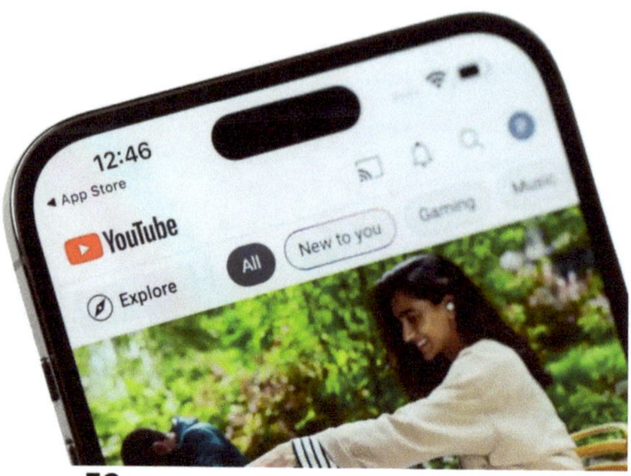

Sharing Photos & Family Group Chats

Your iPhone makes it simple to share memories and stay in touch with your loved ones, whether it's sending a recent picture or chatting in a group message with family.

Sharing Photos with Messages or Mail

To send a photo:

1. Open the **Photos** app
2. Tap the picture you want to send
3. Tap the **Share icon** (box with an arrow pointing up)
4. Choose how to share:

- **Messages**
- **Mail**
- **WhatsApp**
- **AirDrop** (if nearby devices are Apple)

Add a short message if you want, then tap **Send**.

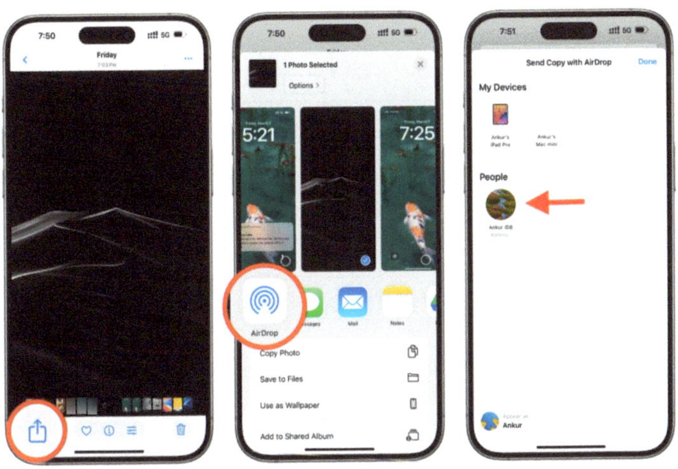

Tip: You can also select multiple photos by tapping Select in the top right corner, then choosing the ones you want to share.

The iPhone 17 Pro makes sharing quick and easy with enhanced performance, ensuring that even large photo libraries and high-res images are processed smoothly.

Creating a Family Group Chat (iMessage)

1. Open the **Messages** app
2. Tap the **Compose icon** (square with pencil)
3. In the **To**: field, enter the names or numbers of your family members
4. Type your message and tap **Send**

Once the message is sent, you'll see the entire group in one conversation. Any replies will appear in the same thread.

Naming the Group and Adding a Photo

1. Open the group message
2. Tap the **top of the screen** (where the group members are listed)
3. Tap **Change Name and Photo**
4. Choose a group name (like "Family Chat") and an image or emoji
5. Tap **Done**

Now everyone will see the name and image at the top of the chat.

Group chats are perfect for sharing updates, birthday photos, daily messages, or planning get-togethers. Group chats are perfect for sharing updates, birthday photos, daily messages, or planning get-togethers. With iPhone 17 Pro's longer battery life, you can chat for hours without needing to recharge, ensuring you're always in touch.

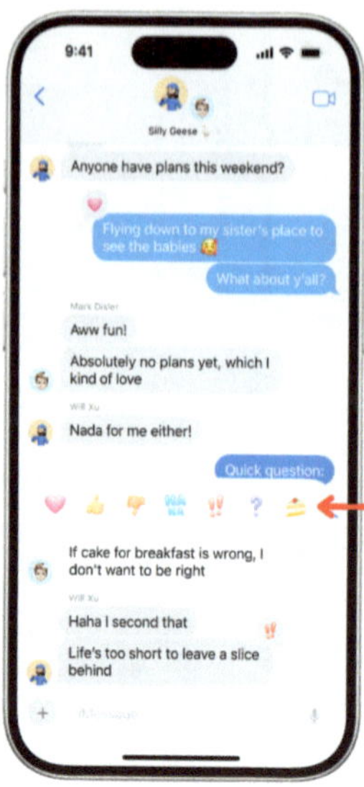

You can even react to messages by holding your finger on one and selecting a thumbs-up, heart, or exclamation point.

Chapter 6: Essential Apps & Tools

Using the Weather & Maps Apps

Your iPhone comes with built-in apps to help you plan your day and get where you're going. Two of the most useful are **Weather** and **Maps**.

Checking the Weather

1. Open the **Weather** app (blue icon with a white cloud and sun)
2. The main screen shows the weather in your current location
3. You'll see:

- Temperature
- Conditions (sunny, cloudy, rain)
- Hour-by-hour forecast
- 10-day outlook
- Sunrise, sunset, wind, humidity, and more

Swipe up to see full details.

To add more cities:

- Tap the list icon in the bottom right
- Tap the plus (+) sign
- Type the name of the city you want to add
- Tap to select and view its forecast

You can switch between cities anytime and get alerts for severe weather. With **iPhone 17 Pro**, **AI-powered weather alerts** keep you informed with predictive warnings, like severe weather and wildfire smoke notifications, ensuring you stay prepared for any conditions.

Using the Maps App for Directions

1. Open the **Maps** app (white icon with a colorful map)
2. Tap the **Search bar** and enter a destination (address or name)
3. Tap **Directions**
4. Choose how you want to get there:

- **Driving**
- **Walking**
- **Transit**
- **Cycling**

5. Tap **Go** to start navigation

The Maps app gives turn-by-turn voice directions and adjusts in real time for traffic. You can also tap **Share ETA** to let someone know when you'll arrive.

With the iPhone 17 Pro's dual-frequency GPS, navigation is even more precise, ensuring accurate directions, especially in crowded areas or places with limited GPS signals. The GPS is also useful for augmented reality (AR) features, giving you a more seamless experience when using location-based apps.

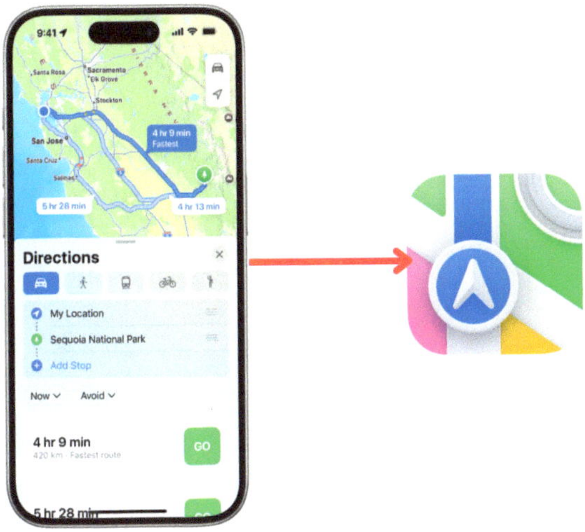

Notes, Calendar & Reminders

Your iPhone includes powerful tools to help you remember things, stay organized, and keep track of your schedule, all without needing paper or sticky notes.

Using the Notes App

1. Open the **Notes app** (yellow and white icon)
2. Tap the **Compose icon** (square with pencil) to start a new note
3. Type or use **voice dictation** to record your thoughts
4. Tap **Done** when finished

You can also:

- Add **checklists** for grocery or to-do lists
- Insert **photos**, **scanned documents**, or **drawings**
- Create folders to keep your notes organized

For better organization, #tags allow you to categorize notes, and you can filter them automatically into Smart Folders. Additionally, any audio recordings made within the Notes app are automatically transcribed into text.

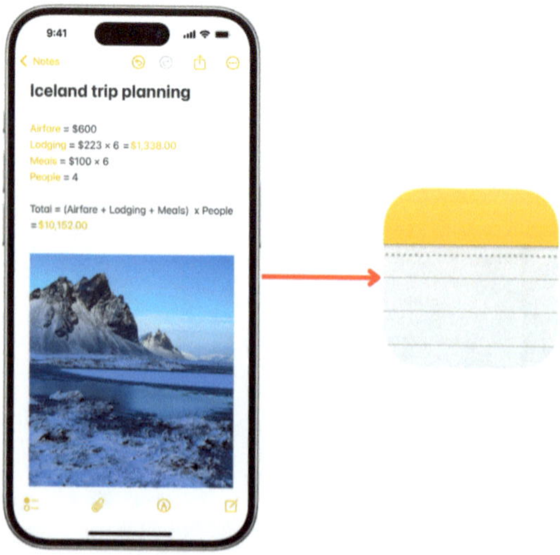

Using the Calendar App

1. Open the **Calendar app** (white icon with the date)
2. Tap the **plus sign** (+) to add a new event
3. Enter a **title, time, location**, and any **alerts** you want
4. Tap **Add** to save it

You can view your schedule by **day, week,** or **month**, and set repeating events for things like birthdays or appointments.

Using the Reminders App

1. Open the **Reminders app** (white icon with three colored dots: blue, red, and orange)
2. Tap **New Reminder**
3. Type your task (e.g., "Pick up prescription")
4. Tap the **"i" icon** to:

- Set a date and time
- Choose a location-based reminder (like when you arrive home)
- Add notes or priority

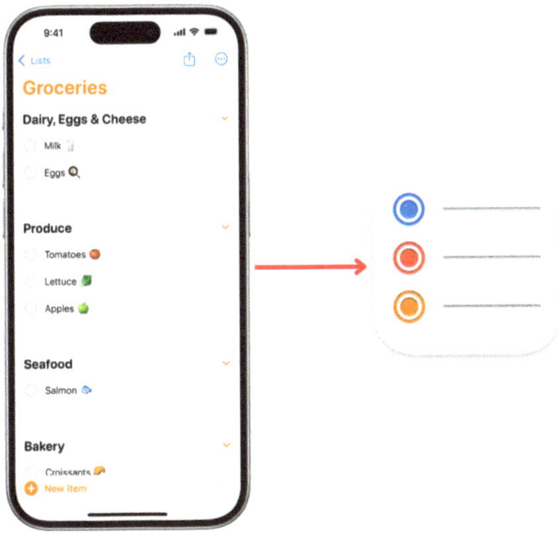

You can organize reminders into lists, check them off when done, and share them with others.

These apps help you stay on top of your tasks, big or small. Whether it's a doctor's visit, a family dinner, or just remembering to water the plants, your iPhone is here to help.

Using Voice Memos & Journal App (iOS 26)

Sometimes, it's easier to speak than to type. Or you might want to reflect on your day in a private space. That's where **Voice Memos** and the new **Journal app** come in.

Voice Memos: Your Digital Recorder

The Voice Memos app lets you record anything, from quick personal reminders to longer conversations or ideas you don't want to forget.

1. To record a voice memo:
2. Open the **Voice Memos app** (black icon with a red and white waveform separated by a vertical blue line)
3. Tap the red record button to begin
4. Tap again to pause or stop
5. Your recordings appear in a list below
6. Tap a recording to **rename, trim**, or **share** it

You can also start recording hands-free by saying, "Record a voice memo" to Siri. Recordings are saved automatically and can be organized into folders for easy access. The app is designed to capture clear sound using all available microphones and quietly reduce background noise, so your voice comes through clearly even in busy environments. If you like quick access, the Action Button can be set to start a recording instantly with a single press.

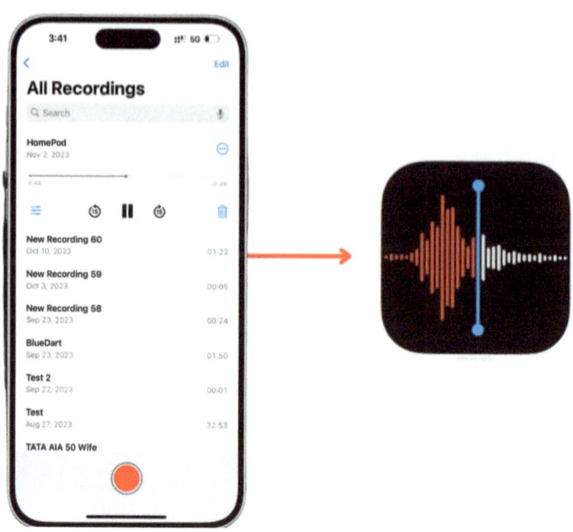

Journal App: A Private Space to Reflect

The Journal app in iOS 26 gives you a simple, private place to capture thoughts, memories, and moments from your day.

To start journaling:

1. Open the **Journal app** (dark icon with a butterfly-like shape in purple, pink, and red gradients)
2. Tap the **plus** (+) button to begin a new entry
3. You can:
- **Write a note**
- **Add photos or locations**
- **Include people or activities from your day**
4. Tap **Done** to save

Helpful suggestions may appear to inspire you, such as a recent walk, a photo you took, or an interaction from earlier in the day, making journaling feel natural rather than forced. All entries are private, protected by Face ID, and stored securely so only you can access them.

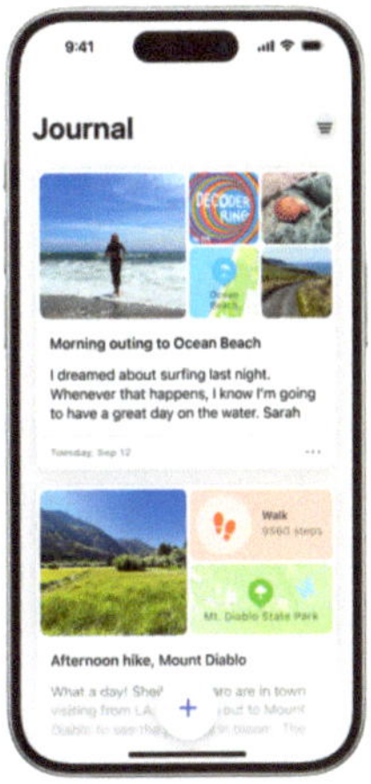

Apple Translate & Real-Time Conversations

The **Translate app** on your iPhone helps you speak and understand other languages in real time. Whether you're traveling, chatting with someone from another country, or learning a new language, this tool makes communication smoother and more natural.

Using the Translate App

1. Open the **Translate app** (gray icon with two speech bubbles, one with an "A")
2. At the top of the screen, choose the **two languages** you want to translate between (for example, English and Spanish)
3. Tap inside the text box and **type** a sentence to translate
4. Or tap the microphone icon to **speak** the sentence aloud
5. The translation will appear on screen and can also be spoken aloud by the app

You can **swap the languages** at any time using the **arrow button** between them.

Conversation Mode

This mode lets two people speak into the phone one at a time, and it will translate both sides automatically.

To use Conversation Mode:

1. Open the Translate app and select your languages
2. Tap the **Conversation icon** at the bottom (it looks like two microphones)
3. Begin speaking. Your iPhone will detect which language is being used and display both sides of the conversation
4. Translations appear on screen and are spoken aloud

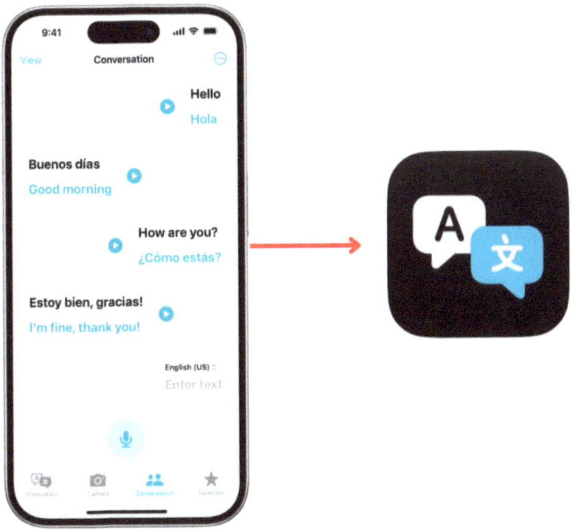

You can use Conversation Mode in either **portrait** or **landscape** view. Landscape gives a split-screen look, but it works perfectly upright too.

Offline Translations

No internet? No problem.

1. Tap the **language name**
2. Tap the **download icon** next to the language you want to use offline

This is especially helpful when traveling without mobile data.

The Translate app brings people together by breaking down language barriers. It's one of the easiest tools to use and one of the most powerful for connecting across cultures.

Using the App Store & Downloading Apps

The App Store is where you go to download new apps, update existing ones, and discover tools that make your iPhone more useful. From games and entertainment to health, education, and finance, there's an app for nearly everything.

How to Open the App Store

Look for the **blue icon** with a white "A" made of three lines. Tap it to open. At the bottom of the screen, you'll see four tabs:

- **Today:** Featured apps and stories
- **Games:** Popular and new games
- **Apps:** Categories like health, photo editing, productivity
- **Arcade**: Ad-free games you can play with a subscription
- **Search:** Where you can find any app by name or keyword

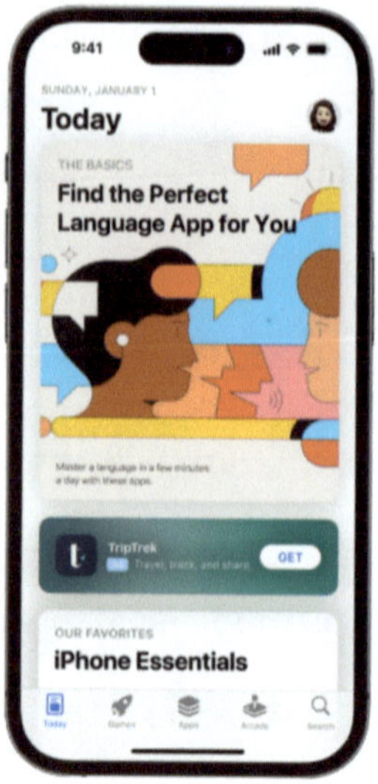

How to Download an App

1. Tap **Search** at the bottom right
2. Type the name of the app (like "Zoom" or "Spotify")
3. Tap the **Get** button next to the app you want
4. Use **Face ID** or enter your **Apple ID** password to confirm
5. The app will download and appear on your Home Screen

If the app says **Open**, that means you already have it installed.

Updating Apps

1. Tap your **profile icon** in the top right corner of the App Store
2. Scroll down to see a list of apps with available updates
3. Tap **Update All** or update apps individually

Keeping apps updated helps them run smoothly, adds new features, and improves security. Updates can also happen automatically in the background, so you don't always have to manage them yourself.

Managing Subscriptions

Many apps are free to download but offer subscriptions. To manage them:

1. Open **Settings**
2. Tap your **Apple ID** name at the top
3. Tap **Subscriptions**
4. View, cancel, or change any active subscriptions

Your iPhone becomes more useful with the right apps. Whether you want to relax, learn something new, stay connected, or get organized, the App Store gives you endless options to explore at your own pace.

Chapter 7: Privacy, Security & Safety

Your iPhone includes powerful tools to help protect your privacy, guard against scams, and keep your personal information secure. Most of these features are built in and easy to manage, even if you're new to smartphones.

Setting a Passcode & Using Face ID

Your passcode is your first line of defense.

To change or set a passcode:

1. Go to **Settings** > **Face ID** & **Passcode**
2. Enter your current passcode if prompted
3. Tap **Change Passcode** or **Turn Passcode On**
4. Choose a 6-digit code, or tap **Passcode Options** for other formats

Face ID lets you unlock your phone quickly and securely. You can also use it for apps, purchases, and filling in saved passwords.

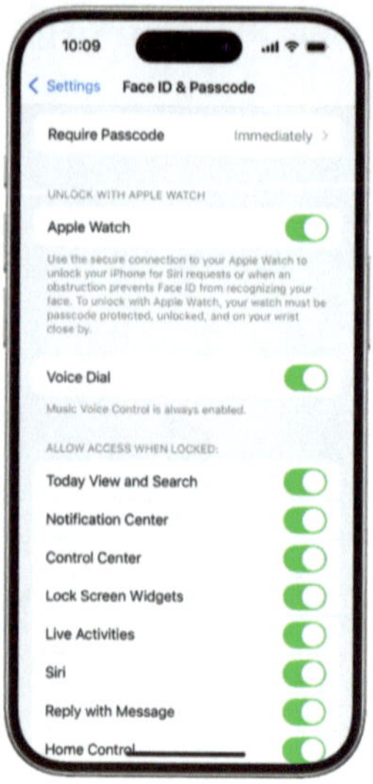

Controlling App Privacy

You can decide what information each app can access.

To manage app permissions:

1. **Open Settings** > **Privacy & Security**
2. Tap any category (e.g., Location Services, Contacts, Microphone)

3. Review which apps have access
4. Tap an app to allow or deny permission

Apps must ask for your approval before accessing sensitive features like your camera or photos.

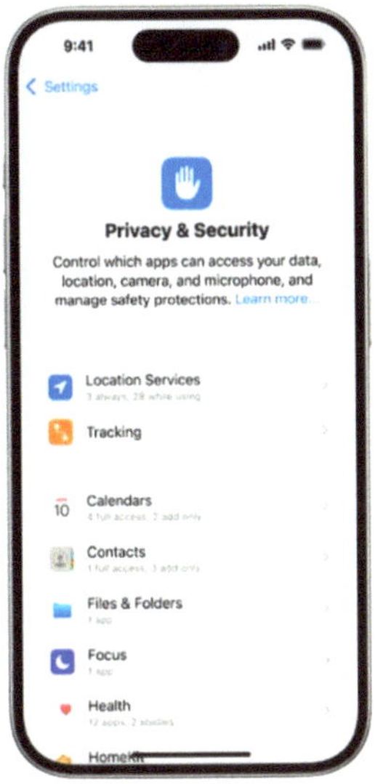

Reviewing App Privacy Reports
iPhone can show you how apps behave in the background.

1. Go to **Settings** > **Privacy & Security** > **App Privacy Report**
2. Turn it on
3. After some use, you'll see:
- Which apps access your data
- How often they use it
- What websites they contact

This makes it easier to spot apps that may be using more information than expected.

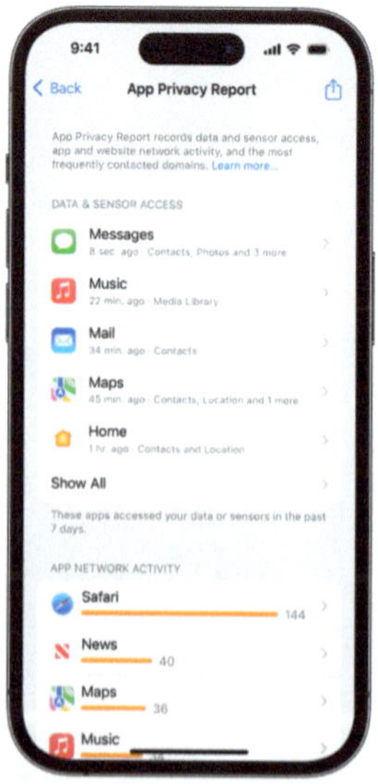

Safety Check: For Emergencies or Abuse Situations

If you're ever in a situation where you need to quickly stop sharing your location, messages, or personal data, **Safety Check** lets you do this in just a few taps.

To use Safety Check:

1. Go to **Settings** > **Privacy & Security** > **Safety Check**
2. Choose **Emergency Reset** to instantly stop sharing with all people and apps
3. Or use **Manage Sharing & Access** to review and stop sharing with specific people or apps one by one

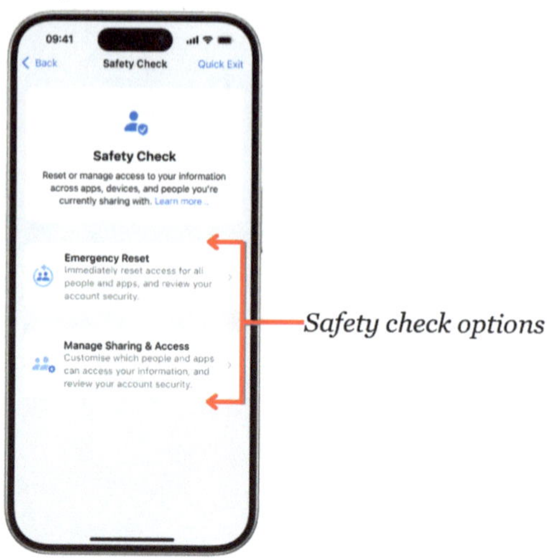

This tool also lets you review blocked contacts and see what information is being shared, all in one place. It's especially helpful if you feel unsafe or need to regain control of your privacy quickly.

Lockdown Mode (High Security Option)

Lockdown Mode is designed for people who believe they may be targeted by advanced cyber threats. It limits certain features to reduce the risk of hacking or spying.

To enable it:

1. Go to **Settings** > **Privacy & Security** > **Lockdown Mode**
2. Tap **Turn On Lockdown Mode**
3. Restart your iPhone when prompted

Most people will never need this feature, and that's okay. It's meant only for very specific situations, such as journalists or individuals facing serious digital threats.

Your iPhone works quietly in the background to protect you, but knowing where these tools are gives you more confidence and control when it matters most.

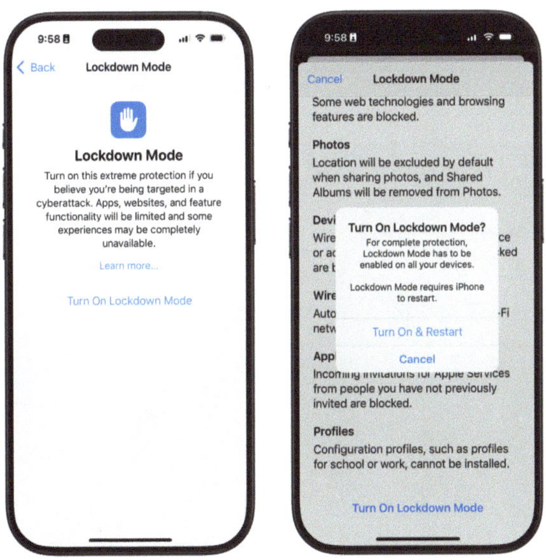

Chapter 8: Apple Wallet & Payments

The **Wallet app** on your iPhone 16 Pro lets you carry credit and debit cards, transit passes, event tickets, and more, all in one secure place.
It also enables **Apple Pay**, so you can make quick, contactless payments using just your phone.

Setting Up Apple Wallet

1. Open the **Wallet app** (black icon with a stack of colorful cards)

2. Tap the **plus sign** (+) in the top right corner
3. Follow the prompts to add:

- **Credit or debit cards**
- **Transit cards**
- **Digital IDs** (in supported regions)
- **Event or movie tickets** (from participating apps or emails)

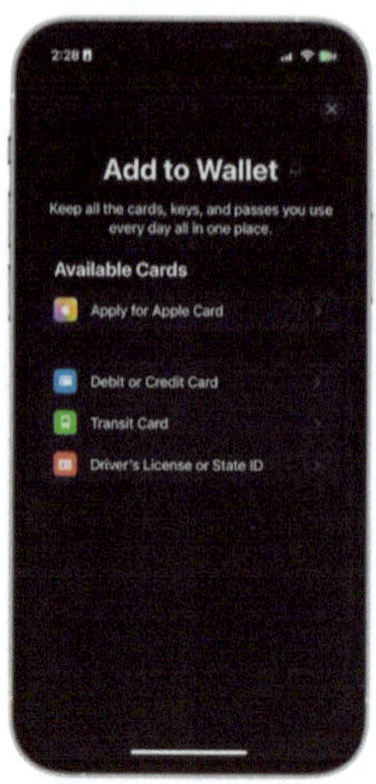

Once a card or pass is added, you can access it directly from the **Lock Screen** or by **double-clicking** the **Side button**.

Tickets stored in Wallet can be used seamlessly for entry, rides, and purchases at supported locations, including large venues and theme parks, without needing to open another app.

Using Apple Pay for Contactless Payments

Apple Pay works at stores, vending machines, restaurants, and websites.

To pay with Face ID:

1. **Double-click** the Side button
2. Glance at your iPhone to confirm with Face ID
3. Hold the top of your iPhone near the payment terminal
4. You'll feel a tap and hear a chime when the payment goes through

No need to unlock your phone or open an app.

Tap to Cash and Peer Payments

With **Tap to Cash**, you can send or receive money by simply holding two iPhones close together. This is helpful for splitting bills or paying someone quickly without exchanging details.

You can also use **Apple Cash** in Messages:

1. Open a conversation
2. Tap the **Apple Cash** button
3. Enter an amount
4. Tap **Send**, then confirm with Face ID

Funds go straight to the recipient's Apple Cash balance and can be used immediately.

Managing Your Wallet

1. Go to **Settings** > **Wallet & Apple Pay** to:

- Choose a default card
- Enable Express Transit
- Manage your billing address and shipping info
- Toggle Apple Pay on or off for certain cards

You can also view your recent Apple Pay transactions inside **Wallet** under each card.

Your Wallet app is secure, encrypted, and protected by Face ID. If your phone is ever lost, you can pause or remove cards remotely using **Find My iPhone**.

Sending/Receiving Apple Cash & Tap to Pay

Apple Cash lets you **send**, **receive**, and **spend money** right from your iPhone. Whether you're splitting a lunch bill or sending birthday money, it's quick and easy.

What Is Apple Cash?

Apple Cash is like a digital debit card stored in your Wallet. You can use it to:

1. Pay in stores or online with Apple Pay
2. Send or receive money in Messages
3. Transfer money to your bank account

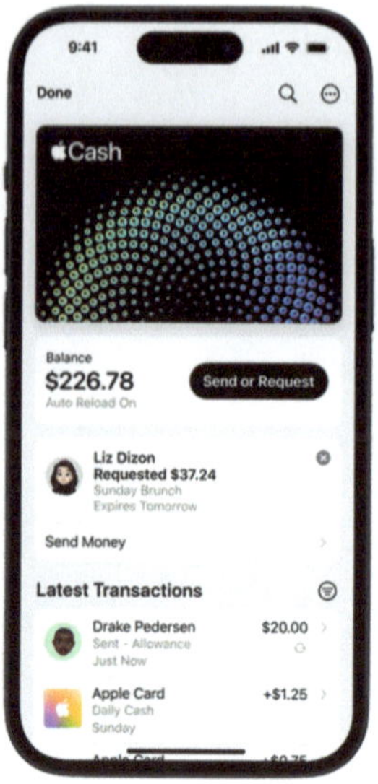

Sending Money with Apple Cash

1. Open the **Messages** app
2. Start a conversation with the person you want to send money to
3. Tap the **Apple Cash** icon above the keyboard
4. Enter the amount
5. Tap **Pay**, then **Send**
6. Confirm with **Face ID**

The money will go straight to the recipient's Apple Cash balance.

Receiving Money
If someone sends you money:

- You'll get a notification and see the amount added to your Apple Cash balance
- You can leave it in Apple Cash or transfer it to your bank

To transfer money:

1. Open the **Wallet app**
2. Tap your **Apple Cash card**
3. Tap **Transfer to Bank**
4. Enter the amount and confirm

Tap to Pay with Apple Cash
Tap to Cash lets you send or receive money by simply holding two iPhones close together.

1. Open **Wallet**
2. Tap your **Apple Cash card**
3. Tap **Send** or **Request**, then **Tap to Cash**
4. Bring your iPhone close to the other person's iPhone
5. Tap to send or receive funds securely

No phone numbers, no bank details, just tap and go.

Apple Cash is secure, encrypted, and verified through Face ID. There are no hidden fees, and it's a convenient way to manage peer-to-peer payments.

Apple Card, Savings, and Rewards

If you want a credit card built directly into your iPhone, the **Apple Card** offers a seamless and secure experience, complete with cashback rewards and a built-in savings account.

What Is the Apple Card?

Apple Card is a digital-first credit card offered by Apple and Goldman Sachs. It lives inside the **Wallet** app, and you can also request a physical titanium card if you prefer.

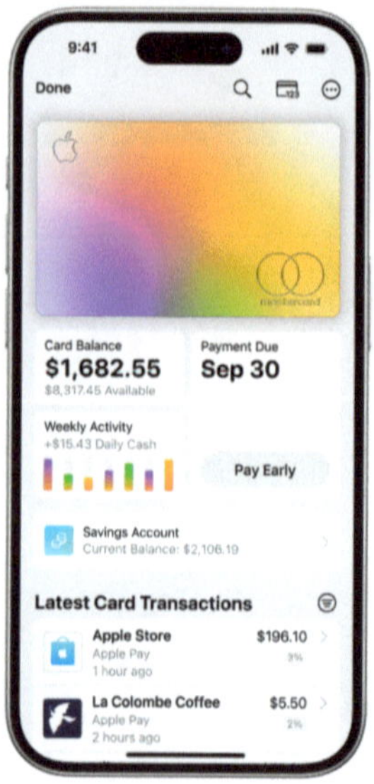

You can apply directly from your iPhone:

1. Open the **Wallet app**
2. Tap the **plus sign** (+)
3. Select **Apple Card** and follow the steps

Approval usually takes just a few minutes, and once approved, you can start using it immediately.

Using Apple Card

- Use it anywhere Apple Pay is accepted
- View spending by category (food, travel, shopping)
- Get daily spending notifications
- Manage payments in the Wallet app with no fees

Your balance, due date, and interest are always clearly shown, making it easy to stay on top of payments.

Daily Cash Rewards

You'll earn **Daily Cash** on every purchase:

- **3% back** on Apple purchases and select merchants
- **2% back** when you use Apple Pay
- **1% back** when using the physical card

Daily Cash is added automatically to your Apple Cash balance, so there's no waiting for monthly rewards.

Apple Card Savings Account

You can also open a **high-yield savings account** directly in Wallet. Any Daily Cash you earn can be deposited there to earn interest.

To set it up:

1. Tap your **Apple Card** in Wallet
2. Tap **Daily Cash**
3. Choose **Set Up Savings** and follow the steps

You can move money in or out anytime, and your savings balance stays visible inside Wallet.

Apple Card is a good option if you want to simplify spending, track finances easily, and earn cash back without juggling multiple apps or paper statements.

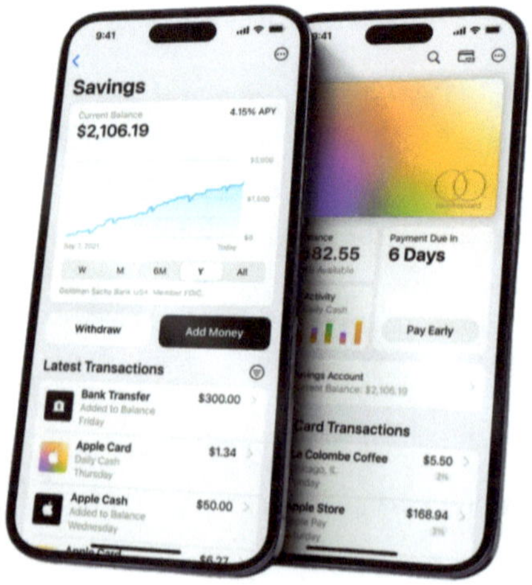

Using Express Mode & Event Tickets

Your iPhone makes everyday tasks like commuting and attending events faster and easier with **Express Mode** and digital tickets in Wallet.

What Is Express Mode?

Express Mode lets you use your iPhone to pay for things like transit, building access, or student ID features **without unlocking your phone.**

To set it up:

1. Open the **Settings** app
2. Tap **Wallet & Apple Pay**
3. Tap **Express Transit Card or Express Mode**
4. Choose the card or pass you want to use automatically

Now, when you hold your iPhone near a compatible reader (like a subway turnstile), it will scan and authorize without needing Face ID or a passcode, even if your phone is asleep.

Tip: Express Mode works even if your iPhone battery is low, thanks to **Power Reserve**.

Using Wallet for Event Tickets

If you bought tickets to a concert, movie, plane, or sports event, you can usually add them to Wallet.

To add a ticket:

- Tap **Add to Apple Wallet** from an email, text, or app
- Follow the on-screen instructions
- Your ticket will appear in the **Wallet app**

To use your ticket at the event:

- Open the **Wallet app**
- Tap the ticket
- Hold your phone near the scanner at the entrance

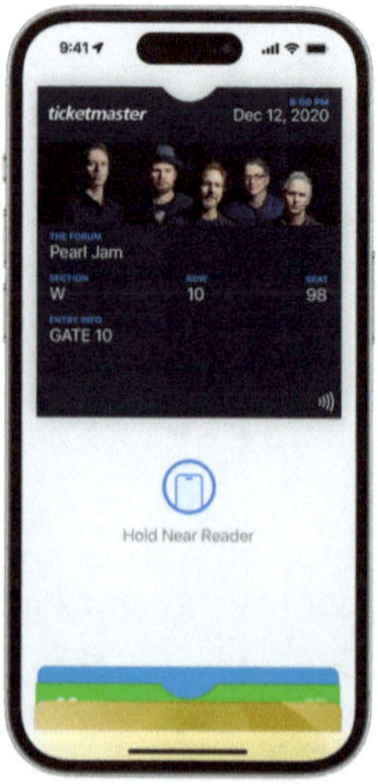

As the event gets closer, your ticket can stay easy to access so you don't have to search for it when you arrive.

Using Wallet keeps things simple. Whether you're catching a train or heading into a concert, everything you need is ready with just a tap.

Chapter 9: Accessibility for Seniors

The iPhone 17 Pro is packed with thoughtful features that make it easier to see, hear, touch, and interact with your device, no matter your age or ability. Apple's Accessibility tools are especially helpful for seniors who want more comfort and less frustration while using their device.

Making Text & Buttons Easier to See

If you ever find yourself squinting at your phone, try these options:

1. Larger Text Sizes

- Go to **Settings** > **Accessibility** > **Display & Text Size** > **Larger Text**
- Enable **Larger Accessibility Sizes** and adjust the slider

2. Bold Text & High Contrast

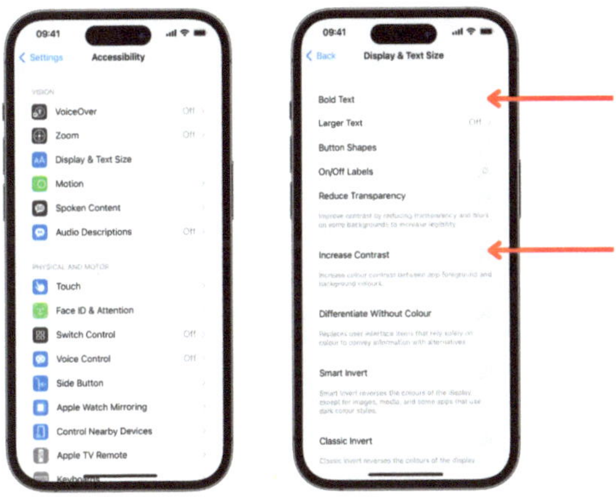

Turn on **Bold Text** to make words thicker and clearer

Try **Increase Contrast** to make screen elements stand out more

3. Button Shapes & Labels

- Enable **Button Shapes** so you can clearly identify where to tap
- Turn on **On/Off Labels** for visible switches (instead of relying on color)

4. Zoom

- Use two fingers to double-tap and zoom into the screen
- Or turn on **Zoom** under Accessibility to use a magnifying glass effect across the screen

Display Accommodations

Dark Mode and **Color Filters** can also reduce eye strain:

- **Dark Mode:**

Go to **Settings** > **Display & Brightness** and choose **Dark**. This replaces bright white backgrounds with softer dark ones.

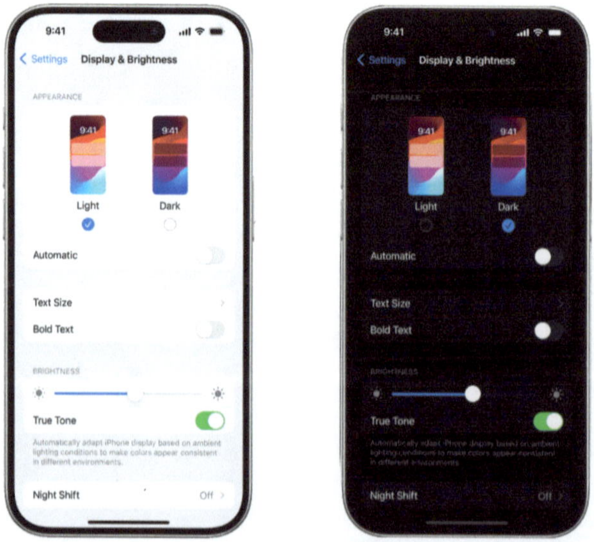

- **Color Filters:**

Helpful for people with color blindness. Go to **Settings** > **Accessibility** > **Display & Text Size** > **Color Filters** to explore different options.

These simple changes make your iPhone more comfortable to use for longer periods and give you greater confidence navigating apps and reading messages.

Using the Magnifier, Voice Control & Live Listen

Apple includes several powerful tools that turn your iPhone into a helpful device for vision, hearing, and mobility support. These features are designed to assist without overwhelming, making your phone easier to use every day.

Magnifier: Your Built-In Digital Glass

The **Magnifier app** uses your iPhone's camera to zoom in on small text, signs, labels, or anything that's hard to read.

To turn on Magnifier:

1. Open **Settings** > **Accessibility** > **Magnifier**
2. Turn on the toggle
3. Open the **Magnifier app** (or triple-press the Side button to launch quickly)

Once open, you can:

- Zoom in with the slider
- Turn on the flashlight for better lighting
- Apply color filters to improve visibility
- Freeze the frame if your hand shakes

Voice Control: Navigate with Your Voice

Voice Control lets you tap, swipe, and type using your voice. No need to touch the screen.

To turn on Voice Control:

1. Go to **Settings** > **Accessibility** > **Voice Control**
2. Tap **Set Up Voice** Control and follow the instructions

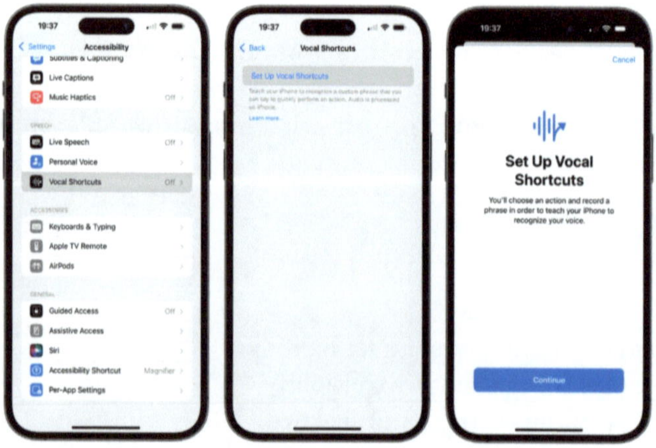

3. Once enabled, say commands like:

- “Open Messages”
- “Swipe left”
- “Tap Send”
- “Go home”

Your phone listens continuously, and you’ll see a blue microphone icon when Voice Control is active.

Live Listen: Hearing Support Through AirPods

If you use AirPods or compatible hearing aids, your iPhone can act like a remote microphone.

To use Live Listen:

1. Open **Settings** > **Control Center**
2. Add **Hearing** to your Control Center
3. Put on your AirPods and open Control Center
4. Tap the **ear icon** and choose **Live Listen**

Now, your iPhone will pick up sounds and transmit them directly to your ears, ideal for conversations in noisy rooms or across a table.

These tools offer more independence and ease without requiring complicated setup. They're designed to support your needs, not change your habits.

Hearing Aid Compatibility & Accessibility Shortcut

The iPhone 17 Pro is built to support a wide range of hearing devices and make accessibility features just a **triple-click away**. These tools give you faster control and better sound, without needing extra apps or complicated menus.

Hearing Aid Compatibility

iPhones are **Made for iPhone (MFi)** hearing aid compatible, meaning they work with many Bluetooth-enabled hearing aids and sound processors.

To pair your hearing aids:

1. Open **Settings** > **Accessibility** > **Hearing Devices**
2. Turn on your hearing aids and place them near the iPhone
3. Tap your device name when it appears
4. Follow the pairing instructions

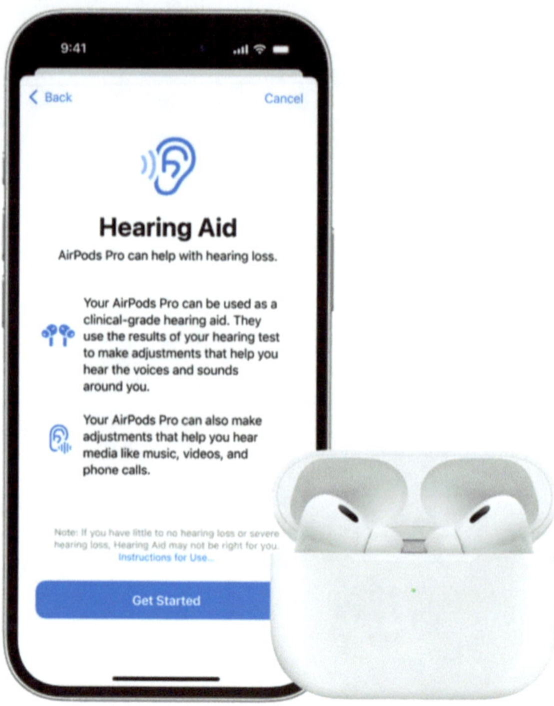

Once paired, you can:

- Adjust volume independently for each ear
- Stream calls, music, and Siri directly into your hearing aids
- Use **Live Listen** as a remote mic for better clarity

You can also check your battery status and audio routing preferences under this menu.

Using the Accessibility Shortcut
You can assign a quick-access shortcut that launches your favorite Accessibility feature when you **triple-click the Side button**.

To set it up:

1. Go to **Settings** > **Accessibility**
2. Scroll down to **Accessibility Shortcut**
3. Choose one or more features (Magnifier, Voice Control, Zoom, etc.)

If you select more than one option, a menu will appear when you triple-click so you can choose what you want to use. This shortcut is especially helpful if you want fast access without digging through settings.

Personal Voice & Custom Assistive Features

Your iPhone includes advanced tools that help you communicate and interact in ways that match your needs, including creating a voice that sounds like you and speaking by typing.

Personal Voice: Your Voice, Digitally Preserved

This feature allows you to create a version of your own voice that can speak aloud for you, helpful for those at risk of losing speech due to conditions like ALS or stroke.

To create a Personal Voice:

1. Go to **Settings** > **Accessibility** > **Personal Voice**

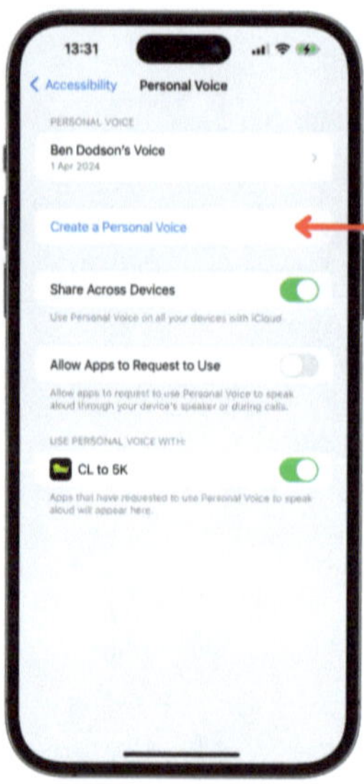

2. Tap to Create a **Personal Voice**

3. Follow the instructions to record about 15–20 minutes of phrases in a quiet room
4. Once complete, your iPhone creates a digital version of your voice

You can then use it with **Live Speech**, typing text and having your custom voice read it aloud in real-time.

Live Speech: Speak by Typing

Live Speech helps you **type messages that are spoken aloud,** whether during a phone call, FaceTime, or in-person.

To turn it on:

1. Go to **Settings** > **Accessibility** > **Live Speech**
2. Turn it on
3. Add commonly used phrases for quick access (like "Please wait a moment" or "Thank you")
4. Triple-click the Side button to activate it anytime

Type your message using the keyboard, and your phone will speak it for you. Live Speech works across apps and appears as a simple overlay, so it's easy to use when needed.

Other Custom Assistive Tools

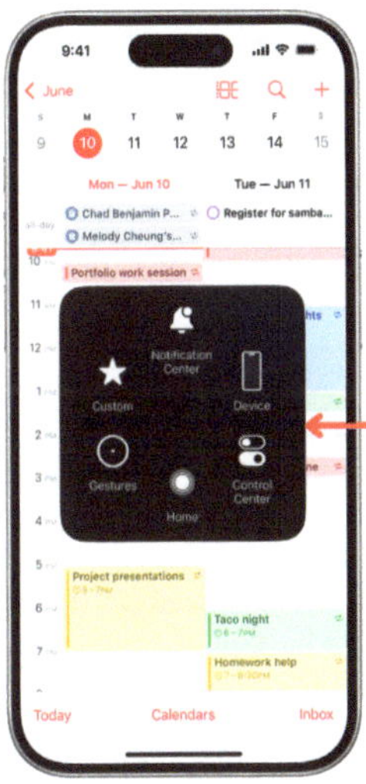

AssistiveTouch: Adds a virtual Home button to your screen for easier navigation

- **Back Tap**: Lets you double or triple-tap the back of your phone to trigger actions like opening the camera or flashlight.
  Go to **Settings** > **Accessibility** > **Touch** > **Back Tap** to set it up
- **Switch Control**: Allows you to control your iPhone with external switches or a single tap, useful for limited mobility

These features allow you to use your phone your way, with more freedom, dignity, and support.

Chapter 10: Troubleshooting Made Easy

Even the best devices can have hiccups. The good news is that your iPhone 16 Pro includes built-in tools and simple steps to fix most common issues on your own; no stress, no tech skills required.

Fixing a Frozen Screen or App Crashes

If your screen becomes unresponsive or an app won't open properly, don't panic. Here's what to do.

1. Force Quit the App

If only one app is acting up:

1. Swipe up from the bottom of the screen and pause in the center
2. You'll see all open apps
3. Swipe left or right to find the app
4. Swipe up on it to close
5. Tap the app again to reopen it

2. Restart Your iPhone

If the whole phone is frozen or slow:

1. Press and hold the **Side button** and either **Volume button** until you see the power slider
2. Slide to power off
3. Wait a few seconds, then press and hold the **Side button** again to turn it back on

A simple restart often clears minor software issues.

3. Check for Software Updates

Updates often fix bugs and improve performance.

1. Go to **Settings** > **General** > **Software Update**
2. If an update is available, tap **Download and Install**

It's a good idea to back up your phone before installing major updates.

4. Delete and Reinstall Problem Apps
Sometimes an app just needs a fresh start.

1. Tap and hold the app icon
2. Tap **Remove App** > **Delete App**
3. Reinstall it from the **App Store**

You won't lose your data if the app uses iCloud or account-based storage.

If none of these steps work, we'll cover more advanced tips and when to seek help in the next pages.

Battery Drain or Slow Performance Fixes

If your iPhone 17 Pro battery is draining too quickly or the device feels sluggish, there are simple ways to improve both speed and battery life. No advanced tech knowledge needed.

Check Battery Usage

1. Open **Settings** > **Battery**
2. Scroll down to see which apps are using the most power
3. Look for apps that run in the background often (like Maps, Mail, or Facebook)

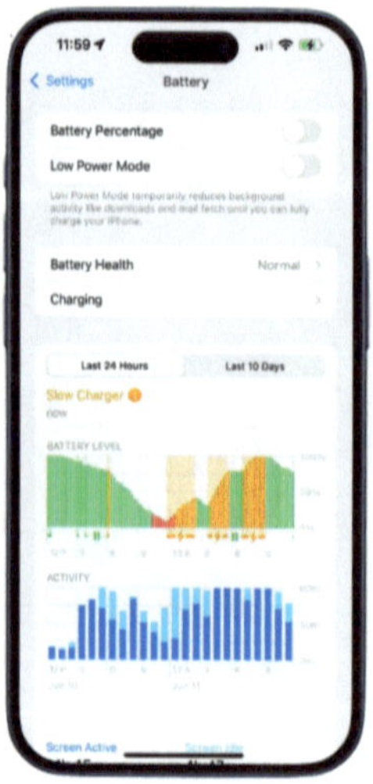

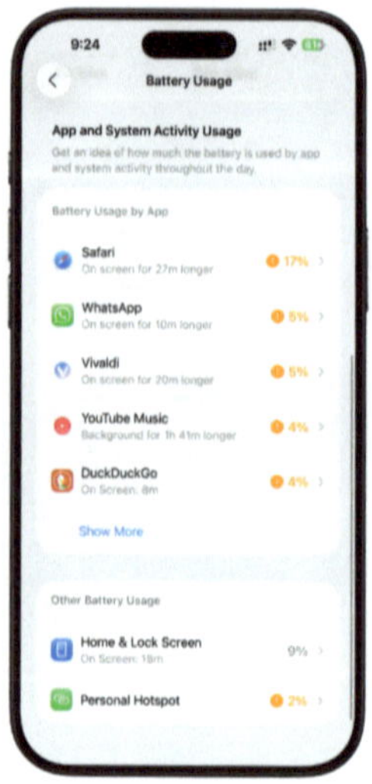

If an app is using too much battery, consider limiting how often you use it or adjusting its notification and background settings.

Enable Low Power Mode

Low Power Mode helps stretch your battery when it's running low by temporarily reducing background activity and screen effects.

1. Go to **Settings** > **Battery**

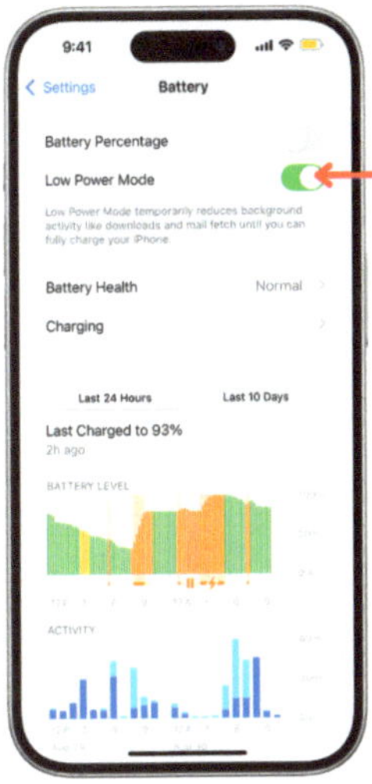

2. Turn on **Low Power Mode**

You'll see a **yellow battery icon** in the top corner. This mode turns off non-essential features like mail fetch, background app activity, and visual effects.

Your phone can also suggest turning this on automatically when the battery reaches 20%, so you don't have to remember to enable it yourself.

Close Background Apps

While iPhones are good at managing background apps, manually closing ones you're not using can help:

1. Swipe up from the bottom of the screen
2. Pause in the center to show open apps
3. Swipe up on apps to close them

Turn Off Unused Features

You can save power by turning off features when not in use:

- **Bluetooth**: Settings > Bluetooth
- **Location Services**: Settings > Privacy & Security > Location Services
- **Raise to Wake**: Settings > Display & Brightness

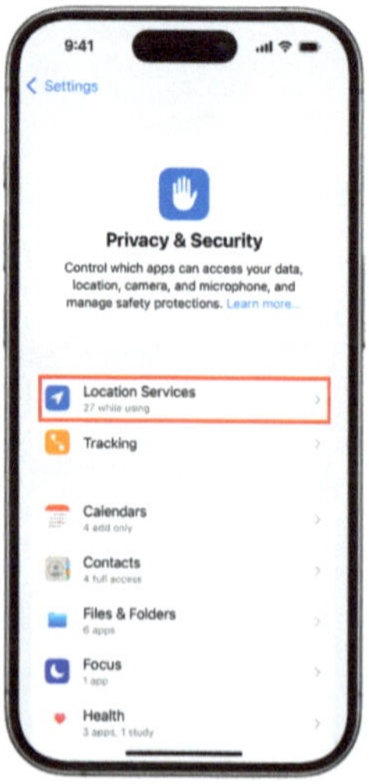

*Slide **left** to turn off Location Services*

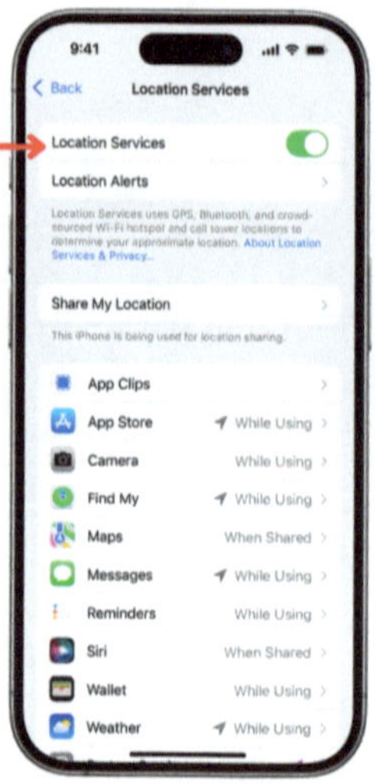

Reduce Motion and Background Effects

1. Go to **Settings** > **Accessibility** > **Motion**
2. Turn on **Reduce Motion** to simplify screen transitions

This simplifies animations, which can improve performance and make the phone feel smoother.

If your phone still feels slow or battery life is very short, we'll cover possible hardware issues and reset options later in the chapter.

Wi-Fi & Network Issues

If your iPhone isn't connecting to the internet, drops Wi-Fi frequently, or struggles with weak signal, don't worry. These simple steps can help you get back online quickly.

1. Check Wi-Fi Settings

1. Open **Settings** > **Wi-Fi**
2. Make sure Wi-Fi is **on**
3. Tap the network you want to join
4. Enter the password if prompted

If you see a **checkmark** next to the network name, you're connected.

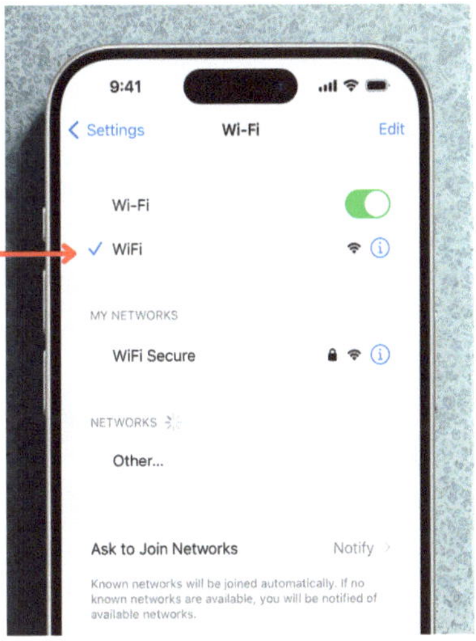

2. Forget and Reconnect to the Network

If you're connected but still having issues:

1. Tap the **"i" icon** next to the network name
2. Tap **Forget This Network**
3. Rejoin by selecting the network and entering the password again

3. Restart Your Router and iPhone

Turn off your home Wi-Fi router, wait 10 seconds, and turn it back on. Then restart your iPhone to reset the connection.

4. Toggle Airplane Mode

1. Swipe down from the top right to open **Control Center**

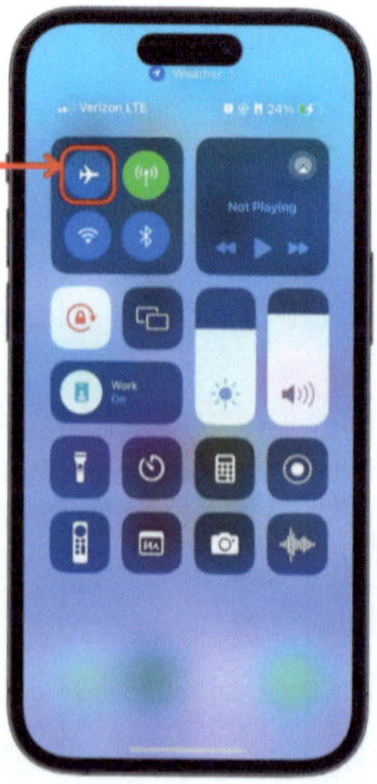

2. Tap the **Airplane Mode** icon to turn it on

3. Wait 5 seconds, then tap it again to turn it off

This refreshes your iPhone's wireless signals, including cellular and Wi-Fi.

5. Reset Network Settings

If nothing else works:

1. Go to **Settings** > **General** > **Transfer or Reset iPhone**
2. Tap **Reset** > **Reset Network Settings**
3. Enter your passcode and confirm

This erases saved Wi-Fi passwords and network settings, but won't delete apps or photos.

If the issue continues after trying these steps, it could be due to an internet outage from your service provider, or your iPhone may need to be checked by a technician.

Resolving App Crashes and Software Update Problems

If apps keep crashing or your phone has trouble updating, these steps usually fix the problem.

Fixing App Crashes

If one app keeps closing on its own or won't open at all:

1. Force Quit and Reopen the App

- Swipe up from the bottom and pause

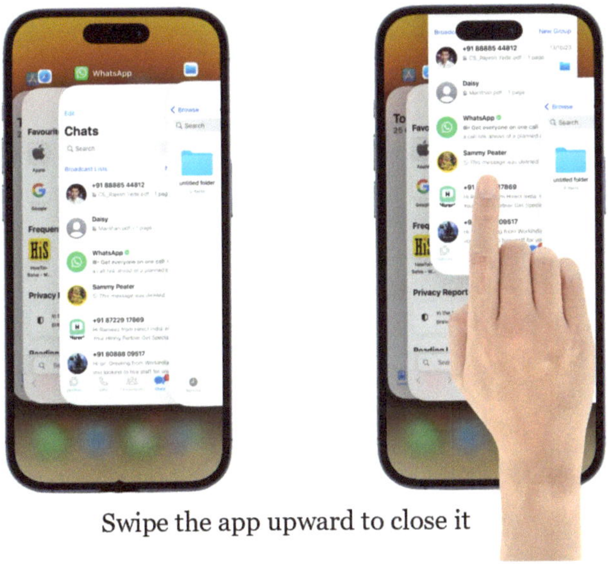

Swipe the app upward to close it

- Reopen the app from the Home Screen

2. Check for App Updates

- Open the **App Store**
- Tap your profile icon (top right)
- Scroll down to see if an update is available
- Tap **Update**

3. Delete and Reinstall the App

- Tap and hold the app
- Tap **Remove App** > **Delete App**
- Reinstall it from the App Store

If the app uses iCloud or account syncing, your data will not be lost.

Fixing Software Update Issues

If your iPhone won't update or gets stuck:

1. Make Sure You Have Enough Storage

- Go to **Settings** > **General** > **iPhone Storage**
- Free up space if storage is nearly full (delete old apps, photos, or large files)

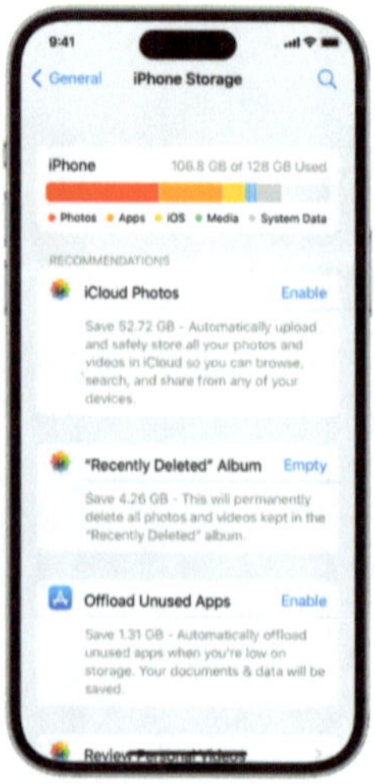

2. Plug In and Connect to Wi-Fi

- Your iPhone must be charging and connected to Wi-Fi for most updates to install
- Go to **Settings** > **General** > **Software Update** to check for updates

3. Restart and Try Again

If the update is stuck, restart your iPhone and go back to the update screen

4. Use a Computer if Needed

- Connect your iPhone to a Mac or PC
- Open Finder (Mac) or iTunes (PC)
- Select your iPhone and click **Check for Update**

Updates keep your phone secure and apps running smoothly, so it's worth keeping your software current. If issues continue, we'll cover when to seek extra help on the next page.

Action Button or Dynamic Island Not Responding

The **Action Button** and **Dynamic Island** are standout features, but like any technology, they may occasionally stop working as expected. Here's how to troubleshoot both.

Fixing Action Button Issues

If your Action Button isn't responding or is triggering the wrong function:

1. Check the Action Button Settings

- Go to **Settings** > **Action Button**
- Make sure the correct action is selected
- Swipe through the options and tap your preferred one
- Test it by pressing and holding the button

2. Restart Your iPhone

- Press and hold the **Side button + Volume button**
- Slide to power off
- Turn the phone back on and try again

3. Check for Physical Blockage

- Make sure your case isn't blocking the button
- Press the button directly to test response

4. Try Another Assigned Action

- Change the action temporarily (e.g., set it to open Camera instead of Flashlight)
- If that works, the issue may be with the original action setup

Fixing Dynamic Island Glitches

The Dynamic Island is the pill-shaped area at the top of your screen that shows live activity (like calls, timers, or music).

If it's not working:

1. Restart the iPhone

- Often clears small display bugs or refresh issues

2. Update iOS

- Go to **Settings** > **General** > **Software Update**
- Install any available updates, as improvements and fixes are often included

3. Check App Compatibility

- Not all apps support Dynamic Island yet
- Try using apps like **Music**, **Timer**, or **Phone** to see if the Island activates

4. Reset All Settings (only if issues persist)

- Go to **Settings** > **General** > **Transfer or Reset iPhone** > **Reset** > **Reset All Settings**
- This will not erase data, but will reset layout, Wi-Fi passwords, and preferences

If the Action Button or Dynamic Island still doesn't respond after these steps, it may be a hardware issue. In that case, consider contacting Apple Support.

Device Overheating & Performance Slowdowns

Your iPhone is designed to run efficiently, but under certain conditions it might feel hot or slow down temporarily.

Why Your iPhone May Overheat

Common causes include:

- Long FaceTime or video calls
- GPS navigation for extended periods
- Playing high-performance games
- Using your phone while it's charging
- Direct sunlight or heat exposure (like in a parked car)

Signs of overheating:

- iPhone feels unusually hot to the touch
- Brightness dims automatically
- Charging slows down or pauses
- Apps lag or close unexpectedly
- A temperature warning appears on screen

How to Cool Down Your iPhone

- **Stop charging** and unplug any accessories
- **Close unused apps** running in the background
- **Move to a cooler environment** or shade
- **Remove the case** if it's trapping heat
- **Avoid gaming or video editing** until the phone cools down

The iPhone will usually regulate itself and return to normal within a few minutes.

Dealing with Slow Performance

If your phone is lagging or slow:

1. Restart the iPhone

- A quick reboot clears temporary memory issues

2. Free up storage space

- Go to **Settings** > **General** > **iPhone Storage**
- Delete unused apps, photos, videos, or large files

3. Turn off background activity

- Go to **Settings** > **General** > **Background App Refresh**
- Set it to **Off** or **Wi-Fi Only**

4. Reduce Motion and Visual Effects

- Go to **Settings** > **Accessibility** > **Motion**
- Turn on **Reduce Motion**

5. Update iOS

- Performance updates and bug fixes are included in every iOS release

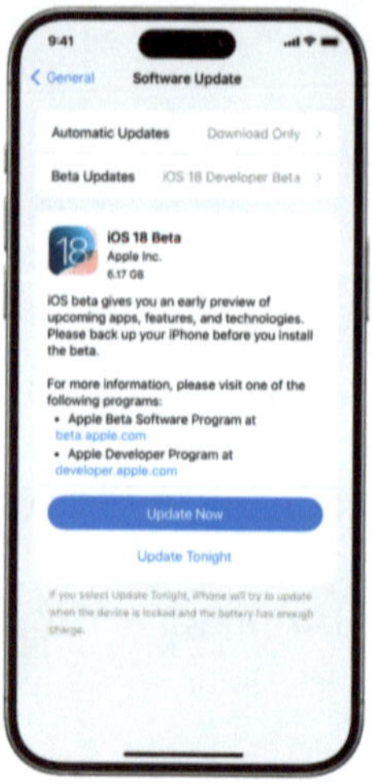

Occasional heat or lag is expected, but repeated slowdowns could signal the need for a more thorough reset or even professional service if hardware is involved.

When to Seek Extra Help or Support

Most iPhone issues can be solved with a simple restart, update, or settings adjustment. But sometimes, it's best to get a little help. Apple offers multiple support options that are senior-friendly and easy to access.

Try the Apple Support App

Download the **Apple Support** app from the App Store. It offers:

- Guided troubleshooting steps
- Chat with an Apple expert
- Appointment scheduling at a nearby Apple Store
- Device coverage details and repair options

Once installed, the app will automatically detect your device model and software version.

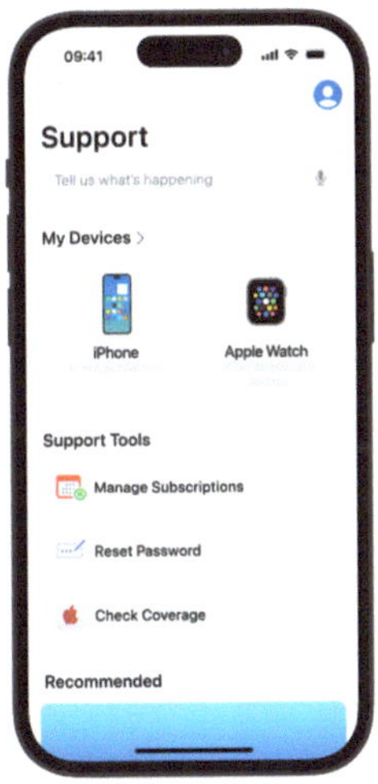

Call Apple Support

You can call Apple Support directly:

Phone (U.S.): 1-800-MY-APPLE (1-800-692-7753)

They will walk you through the issue patiently and offer next steps.

Tip: Write down any error messages or describe the issue clearly to help them assist you faster.

Visit a Genius Bar

If you prefer in-person help:

1. Open the **Apple Support app** or visit getsupport.apple.com
2. Schedule a **Genius Bar appointment**
3. Visit your local Apple Store at the scheduled time

An Apple technician can run diagnostics, repair hardware, or even replace your device under warranty or AppleCare if needed.

Check Your Warranty or AppleCare

To see if your iPhone is still under warranty:

- Go to **Settings** > **General** > **About**
- Tap **Coverage or AppleCare & Warranty**

You can also visit checkcoverage.apple.com and enter your serial number.

Never feel like you have to fix everything yourself. Apple's support system is designed to be approachable and helpful, even if you've never contacted tech support before.

Appendix & Quick Reference

This section includes helpful charts, settings, and quick explanations for everyday use. Whether you're new to the iPhone or just need a refresher, keep these pages bookmarked for fast answers.

Status Icon Chart

Icon	Meaning
	Signal strength (more bars = better connection)
	Wi-Fi connected
	Cellular data active
	Battery level (solid green when charging)
	iPhone is locked
	Silent mode is on
	Focus mode is active
	Sound is on
	Lower power mode is active
	Location services in use
	Alarm is set
	Audio is playing to headphones or AirPods

Your iPhone is sharing its internet connection.

Icons may vary slightly based on apps, accessories, and features you're using.

Button Cheat Sheet

Here's a quick overview of what each button on your iPhone 17 Pro does. It's perfect for reference any time you forget which is which.

Side Button (Right Side)

- **Press Once**: Wake or sleep the screen
- **Press and hold:** Use Siri (if enabled in Settings)
- **Double-Click**: Open Apple Wallet
- **Press with Volume Button**: Bring up the power off screen

Volume Buttons (Left Side)

- **Volume Up / Down**: Control sound level
- **Press Up + Side Button**: Take a screenshot
- **Use in Camera App**: Take a photo or start/stop recording

Action Button (Top Left, above volume)

- Press and hold to trigger a custom action
- Can be set to: Silent Mode, Flashlight, Camera, Voice Memo, Magnifier, Focus Mode, or Accessibility Shortcut

Customize it under: **Settings** > **Action Button**

Face ID Sensor (Front Top Center)

- Automatically scans your face to unlock your phone
- Used for App Store purchases, Apple Pay, and secure login

Having these buttons at your fingertips makes using your iPhone faster and easier, with no guessing required.

Emergency Setup & Medical ID
Your iPhone can help save your life or someone else's by making important health and emergency details available right from the Lock Screen.

Set Up Your Medical ID
Your **Medical ID** stores critical health info such as allergies, medications, blood type, and emergency contacts.

To set it up:

1. Open the **Health app**
2. Tap your **profile photo** in the top right
3. Tap **Medical ID** > Edit
4. Add details like:
   - Name
   - Date of birth
   - Medical conditions
   - Medications
   - Allergies
   - Blood type
   - Emergency contacts
5. Turn on **Show When Locked**
6. Tap **Done**

Now, anyone can view this info by tapping **Emergency** on your Lock Screen, without unlocking your phone.

Set Up Emergency SOS
Emergency SOS lets you call for help quickly, even without unlocking your phone.
To activate SOS:

- **Press and hold the Side button + either Volume button**
- A countdown will begin
- Keep holding to call emergency services automatically
- Or swipe the **SOS slider** on the screen

You can also start Emergency SOS by pressing the Side button five times quickly.

To customize SOS settings:

1. Go to **Settings** > **Emergency SOS**
2. Choose if you want SOS to auto-call
3. Turn on **Call After Severe Crash** if desired

You can also turn on Call Quietly to keep the countdown silent.

Add Emergency Contacts

1. Open the **Health app** > **Medical ID** > **Edit**
2. Scroll to **Emergency Contacts**
3. Tap **Add Contact**
4. Select a contact and their relationship to you
5. Tap **Done**

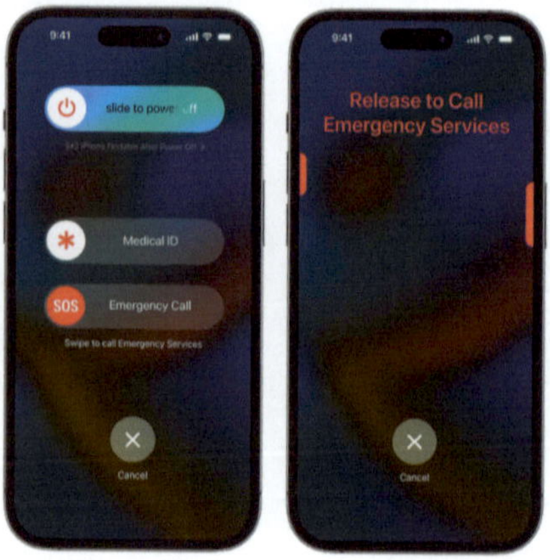

They will be notified automatically when you use Emergency SOS.

Quick Tips: What to Do If Something Goes Wrong

Technology hiccups happen. Here are simple solutions to the most common iPhone problems to get you back on track fast.

If Your iPhone Won't Turn On

- Charge it for at least 10 minutes using a known working cable and adapter
- Press and hold the **Side button** until the Apple logo appears
- Still nothing? Try **Force Restart**:

1. Press and quickly release **Volume Up**
2. Press and quickly release **Volume Down**
3. Press and hold the **Side button** until you see the Apple logo

If You Forgot Your Passcode

You'll need to erase your device and set it up again.
Go to support.apple.com/iphone/passcode for guided instructions.

To avoid this in the future, write down your passcode and keep it somewhere safe.

If You Can't Connect to Wi-Fi

- Toggle **Airplane Mode** on, wait 5 seconds, and turn it off
- Go to **Settings** > **Wi-Fi** and reconnect to your network
- Restart your router and your iPhone
- If needed, **Reset Network Settings** under:
  Settings > **General** > **Transfer or Reset iPhone** > **Reset**

If an App Keeps Crashing

- Force close the app and reopen it
- Check for updates in the **App Store**
- Delete and reinstall the app
- Restart your iPhone

If Your iPhone Feels Slow or Hot

- Close background apps
- Turn on **Low Power Mode**
- Move the phone to a cooler area
- Restart the device
- Update iOS if an update is available

Most problems are easy to solve with a calm approach and a few taps. And if you're unsure, remember that Apple Support is always just one call or visit away.

Glossary: Simple Tech Terms

Not sure what a word means? This glossary explains common iPhone terms in plain language, so you can feel confident while using your phone.

- **App**: A small program that helps you do something on your phone, like send messages or play music
- **App Store**: The place where you download new apps
- **Apple ID**: Your personal login for all Apple services (like iCloud, App Store, and FaceTime)
- **Bluetooth**: A wireless connection used for things like AirPods or speakers
- **Control Center**: A shortcut menu you open by swiping down from the top right of the screen
- **Face ID**: A feature that unlocks your phone by recognizing your face
- **Focus Mode**: A setting that controls who can reach you and which notifications you get
- **iCloud**: Apple's storage service that backs up your photos, contacts, and more online
- **iMessage**: Apple's text messaging system (blue bubbles)
- **Lock Screen**: The first screen you see when you wake your phone
- **Notification**: A small alert or message that pops up on your screen
- **Passcode**: A secret number used to unlock your iPhone
- **Safari**: The iPhone's internet browser
- **Screenshot**: A photo of whatever's currently on your screen
- **Silent Mode**: A setting that turns off ringer and alert sounds
- **Software Update**: A free download that fixes bugs or adds new features
- **Touchscreen**: The glass screen you tap and swipe to use your iPhone
- **Wallet**: An app for storing cards, tickets, and passes
- **Wi-Fi**: A wireless internet connection

Keep this glossary handy any time you need a quick explanation. You've got this!